BROWNIE GIRL SCOUT HANDBOOK

Illustrated

Girl Scouts of the U.S.A.
830 Third Avenue
New York, N.Y. 10022

GIRL SCOUTS OF THE U.S.A.

Betty F. Pilsbury,
President

Frances Hesselbein,
National Executive Director

Inquiries related to the
Brownie Girl Scout Handbook
should be addressed to
Program,
Girl Scouts of the U.S.A.,
830 Third Avenue,
New York, N.Y. 10022.

©1986 by Girl Scouts of the
United States of America
All rights reserved
First Impression May 1986
Printed in the United States of America
Girl Scout Catalog No. 20-787
ISBN 0-88441-337-3

10 9 8 7 6 5 4 3 2 1

CONTENTS

CREDITS

Project Coordinator	Joel E. Becker
Director, Program	Sharon Woods Hussey
Director, Graphics and Design	Michael Chanwick
Authors	Candace White Ciraco
	Sharon Woods Hussey
	Verna L. Simpkins
	Harriet S. Mosatche
	Damariz L. Winborne
Contributors	Cindy Ford
	Toni Eubanks
Design Studio	Keithley and Associates
Cover Design	George Koizumi
Illustrator	Kathy Allert
How-to Illustrator	Betty de Araujo
Editor	David Sahatdjian

GIRL SCOUTING

Welcome to the Girl Scout family. You are a Brownie Girl Scout. Brownie Girl Scouts are six through eight years old or in the first, second, or third grade.

BROWNIE GIRL SCOUTS

As a Brownie Girl Scout, you may be new to Girl Scouting, or you may have joined as a Daisy Girl Scout. There are many ways to be active in Brownie Girl Scouting. You can be a member of a Girl Scout troop or interest group. You can attend a Girl Scout camp or go to Girl Scout council events. You can go to Girl Scout activity centers and be involved in other ways. You will have fun and learn many new things.

USING YOUR BROWNIE GIRL SCOUT HANDBOOK

This handbook is for you to use throughout your Brownie Girl Scout years. You'll find information and activities about the wonderful world of Girl Scouting. You can explore your world, beginning with yourself and continuing to the world around you. This section will help you learn how to use your handbook.

The Worlds of Interest

As a Brownie Girl Scout, there are five exciting worlds of interest for you to explore. In each world, you will learn how to do many things and have fun.

 **The World of Well-Being** will help you learn more about why you are special and how to take care of yourself.

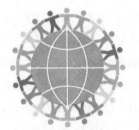 **The World of People** will help you learn about others—your family, friends, troop, school, community, country, and people around the world.

 **The World of Today and Tomorrow** will help you discover how and why things work and what the future holds for you.

 **The World of the Arts** will help you explore things like puppetry, dance, music, pottery, weaving, and painting.

 **The World of the Out-of-Doors** will help you explore the natural world surrounding your troop meeting place, home, community, or camp.

Symbols in the Book

All five worlds have many activities for you to try. These activities can be found throughout the book. Some activities will have this symbol ▲. These activities should be done first. They will prepare you for those with the ◆ symbol.

You will also see in the margin beside each activity a five-sided symbol representing the five worlds of interest. You will know which world of interest the activity belongs to by the color in the symbol.

Following are the colors for each world of interest: the World of Well-Being (red); the World of People (blue); the World of Today and Tomorrow (orange); the World of the Arts (purple); and the World of the Out-of-Doors (yellow). If an activity involves more than one world of interest, the symbol will have more than one color.

There are Brownie Try-Its in each world of interest. Brownie Try-It patches are **recognitions** you receive when you complete a certain number of activities. Look at pages 145–187 for information on Try-Its.

Many parts of the book have places for you to write or draw. If you do not have enough space, attach another piece of paper to the page, as shown in the drawing below. In this way, you will have a record of all your Brownie Girl Scout adventures.

You will also see Suzy Safety throughout the book. She is there to remind you to do things the safe way.

4

THE GIRL SCOUT PROMISE AND LAW

All Girl Scouts make the **Girl Scout Promise**. The words in this Promise are as follows:

On my honor, I will try:
To serve God and my country,
To help people at all times,
And to live by the Girl Scout Law.

These words say a lot about a Girl Scout. Let's look at what a Girl Scout says she will do.

On my honor, I will try This means that a Girl Scout promises to try her best. The words that follow tell what a Girl Scout will try to do.

To serve God There are many ways to serve God. Maybe you will attend religious services and apply religious teachings to your life. You can serve God by trying to live in peace with other people, for example.

▲ Talk with your family or religious leader about ways you can serve God.

◆ Write a story about the ways you serve God.

And my country A Girl Scout serves her country in many ways, including the following: saying the Pledge of Allegiance; taking part in a flag ceremony; being a helpful person in her neighborhood and with her family.

▲ Talk with other Girl Scouts about what serving your country means.

▲ Find pictures that show something interesting about your country.

To help people at all times A Girl Scout tries to help people. Helping someone carry packages is one small way. There are big ways to help, such as taking the time to make something nice for people in the hospital.

▲ Find pictures that show people being helpful.

▲ Make up and act out a play about helping people in your community.

◆ Do your own service project with other Brownie Girl Scouts to help people in some way. A service project is an activity that benefits other people or the community.

To live by the Girl Scout Law   Each part of the Law states a different way to show that you are trying to be the best person you can be. Below each part of the Girl Scout Law are some ways to show that you are trying to live by the Law. Can you think of other ways to live by the Girl Scout Law?

◆ Write them down on the blank lines.

_____

_____

_____

The Girl Scout Law

I will do my best:

To be honest   Tell the truth. Only use a thing that belongs to you unless you have permission from the owner.

_____

_____

_____

To be fair   Share your toys. Let other girls have a chance to play their favorite games.

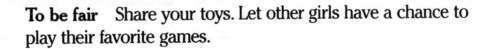

_____

_____

_____

To help where I am needed When you see a job that needs to be done and you can do it, do it. Help make your own lunches if you take your lunch to school.

_____

_____

_____

_____

To be cheerful Help someone feel better if she or he is not happy. Be a good winner or loser when playing games.

_____

_____

_____

_____

To be friendly and considerate Help a friend understand her homework. Ask a new girl to play with you and your friends.

_____

_____

_____

_____

To be a sister to every Girl Scout Help a Girl Scout friend with a project. Help a new girl learn the Girl Scout Promise.

_____

_____

_____

_____

To respect authority Respect your Girl Scout leaders. Obey the law and be cooperative in your home.

_____

_____

_____

_____

To use resources wisely Try not to waste paper. Turn off the lights when leaving a room. Turn off water faucets after you use them.

_____

_____

_____

_____

To protect and improve the world around me   Help in a neighborhood cleanup or planting project. Put litter in trash cans.

_____

_____

_____

_____

To show respect for myself and others through my words and actions   Always try to be the best person you can be. Listen carefully when someone is talking to you.

_____

_____

_____

_____

You may understand some parts of the Girl Scout Law better than others. You may be able to do some parts better than others. One of the best things about being a Girl Scout is that you promise to try.

Girl Scouts and Girl Guides all around the world make a promise like yours. The words may be different, but each one promises to do her very best every day. There are things you can do to find out more about Girl Scouts and Girl Guides in other countries on page 39.

SPECIAL GIRL SCOUT WAYS

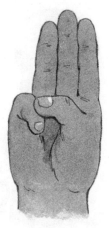

The Girl Scout sign is made when you say the Girl Scout Promise. This special sign is made with the middle three fingers of the right hand raised and the little finger held down by the thumb. The three raised fingers stand for the three parts of the Girl Scout Promise.

The **Girl Scout handshake** is the way Girl Scout friends greet each other. Shake hands with your left hand while giving the Girl Scout sign with your right hand.

The **friendship circle** — Girls stand in a circle. Each girl crosses her right hand over her left. Then she holds hands with the person standing on either side of her.

Friendship squeeze — One person in the friendship circle starts the friendship squeeze. When you feel your hand squeezed, you do the same to the person next to you. Everyone is silent as the friendship squeeze is passed. It stands for friendship with Girl Scouts everywhere.

"Be prepared" is the **Girl Scout motto**. Girl Scouts try to be ready to help when they are needed. They try to be ready for emergencies and able to take care of themselves.

◆ Talk about ways you can be prepared. Write out your ideas below, or have someone help you write them.

1 _____

2 _____

13

"Do a good turn daily" is the **Girl Scout slogan**. It means that each day a Brownie Girl Scout will be helpful, kind, and considerate. Even the smallest act can be very helpful. Can you think of some ways to do a good turn?

◆ Write them here:

1 _____

2 _____

The **quiet sign** is a way to let everyone know it is time to be quiet. Someone raises her right hand. Each person who sees this sign stops talking and raises her hand until there is quiet.

The "Brownie Smile Song" is the Brownie Girl Scouts' special song. Try singing it with your troop.

Brownie Smile Song

1. I've some-thing in my pock-et; it be-longs a-cross my face. And I keep it ver-y close at hand in a most con-ven-ient place.

2. I'm sure you couldn't guess it
If you guessed a long, long while.
So I'll take it out and put it on--
It's a great big Brownie Smile!

Used by kind permission of Harriet F. Heywood.

14

The **Brownie Story** tells how Brownie Girl Scouts got their name. Here is one version of the story.

The Brownie Story

Once upon a time, a little girl and boy named Mary and Tommy lived in a village in the North Country of old England. They lived with their father and grandmother. Their father was a poor tailor who worked very hard all day. Their grandmother was too old to do housework. Still, Mary and Tommy didn't help them very much. They just played all day.

At the end of a hard day's work, the tailor tried his best to keep the house clean. He swept the stone floor and washed the dishes. He brought in wood and made the fire.

"Children are hard to care for," said the tailor one day as he sat at work.

"Children are a blessing!" said the grandmother.

"Ah, not my children," said the tailor. "What they take out to play with, they lose. What they bring in to play with, I have to clean up. And they do not help me a bit."

Just then the door flew open. Mary and Tommy ran in. Their arms were full of sticks and moss, which they threw on the floor.

"Take that rubbish outside," said the tailor. "I've swept this floor once today, and I will not do it again!"

Mary said, "Tommy, you take it out," and sat down near her grandmother. Tommy kicked the moss across the room. Some flew out the door, but the rest scattered over the floor.

"And those sticks, too!" the tailor said as he walked out.

"You pick them up, Mary," said Tommy. "What makes Father so angry, Granny?"

"He is tired, my dear, and you two do not help him."

"What could we do, Granny?"

"Many little things, if you tried. Ah, what this house needs is a brownie or two. The luck of our house left when the brownie left us."

"What is a brownie, Granny?"

"A very helpful little person, my dear."

"What did she do?"

"She was a big help. The brownie came in before the family was up and did all sorts of work. She swept the floor, set the table for breakfast, and tidied the room. The brownie always ran off before anyone could see her. But they could hear her laughing and playing about the house sometimes."

"What a nice brownie! Did they pay her, Granny?"

"No, my dear. Brownies always help for love. But the family left a pan of clear water for her at night. And now and then, they left her a bowl of bread and milk or cream. She liked that."

"Tell us more about the brownies, please," said Mary. "Did they ever live with anybody else?"

"There are plenty of brownies," said the old lady, "or used to be a long time ago. Some houses had several."

"Oh, Granny! Where are they now?"

"Only the Wise Old Owl knows, my dear."

"Who is the Wise Old Owl, Granny?"

"I don't exactly know, my dear."

"Oh, I wish ours would come back," Mary and Tommy said together.

"She'd — "

" — tidy the room," said Mary.

" — wash the dishes," said Tommy.

" — bring in wood for the fire," said Mary.

" — sweep the floor," said Tommy.

" — do everything!"

"Oh, I wish she hadn't gone away! May we put out some bread and milk for her? Maybe she will come back if we do," said Mary.

"Well, well," said the grandmother. "She's welcome, if she chooses to come. There's plenty of work for her to do here."

So Mary and Tommy put out a pan and filled it with bread and milk. Then they went off to bed.

That night Mary could hardly sleep. She kept thinking about the brownie. "There's an owl living in the old shed by the pond," she thought. "It might be the Wise Old Owl herself. If it is, she can tell me where to find a brownie. When Father's gone to bed and the moon rises, I'll go look for the Wise Old Owl."

The moon rose and Mary went outside. She hurried to the pond in the woods. All was still, so still that Mary could hear her heart beating.

Then suddenly, "Hoo! Hoo!" said a voice behind her.

"It's an owl!" said Mary. "Maybe it's the one I'm looking for." The owl flew by her and into the shed by the pond. The old owl sat on a beam that ran under the roof of the shed.

"Come up! Come up!" said the owl.

The owl could talk! Then it must be the Wise Old Owl! Mary climbed up the beam, and sat face to face with the owl.

"Now, what do you want?" said the owl.

"Please," said Mary, "where can I find a brownie to come and live with us?"

"Oohoo!" said the owl. "That's it, is it? I know of two brownies."

"Hurrah!" said Mary. "Where do they live?"

"In your house," said the owl.

"In our house! Then why don't they help us?"

"Perhaps they don't know what has to be done," said the owl.

"Just tell me where to find those brownies," said Mary. "I can show them what has to be done."

"Can you?" said the owl. "Oohoo!" Mary was not sure whether the owl was hooting or laughing.

"Of course I can," she said. "There is plenty to do at our house!"

"Well, Mary, I can tell you how to find one of the brownies. Go to the north side of the pond in the woods when the moon is shining. Turn yourself around three times while you say this charm:

'Twist me and turn me and show me the elf.
I looked in the water and saw _____,'

"Then look into the pond to see the brownie. At the very same time that you see the brownie, you will think of a word that ends the magic rhyme."

Off went Mary, and in no time she reached the edge of the still, dark pond. Like a mirror, the pond reflected the shining moon.

18

Mary stood at the north side. Then, slowly, she turned herself round three times while she said the rhyme:

"Twist me and turn me and show me the elf.
I looked in the water and saw _____"

Then she stopped and looked into the pond. There she saw—only her own face.

"How silly," said Mary. "I must have done it wrong." She looked in again. "There's no word to rhyme with elf, anyway. Belf! Helf! Jelf! Melf! How silly! And then to look for a brownie and see nothing but myself! Myself? Myself? But that does rhyme with elf! And it's just what I did, too. How very odd! Something must be wrong. I'll go back and ask the Wise Old Owl about it."

So Mary went back to the shed and climbed up beside the old owl.

"Whoooo," said the owl, "and what did you see in the pond?"

"I saw nothing but myself," said Mary.

"And what did you expect to see?" asked the owl.

"A brownie," said Mary. "You told me so."

"And what are brownies like?" inquired the owl.

"Granny says brownies are very helpful little persons."

"Ah!" said the owl, "and the one you saw was not? Are you sure you did not see a brownie?"

"Yes," said Mary. "I saw no one but myself. I'm not a brownie."

"Are you quite sure?" asked the owl again. "All children can be brownies. Couldn't you sweep the floor, set the table, fetch the wood and water, tidy the room, and pick up your own things?"

"I don't think I would like it," Mary said. "I'd rather have a brownie do it for me."

"And what would you be doing meanwhile?" asked the owl. "You would be someone who never helps—who makes work instead of doing it!"

"Oh, no!" cried Mary, "I don't want to be like that. I'll go home and tell Tommy and we'll both try to be brownies."

"That's the way to talk!" said the owl. "Come on, I'll take you home."

Before Mary knew it, she was in her own little bed.

Mary could hardly wait for daylight to come. She woke up Tommy and told him what had happened. Together they crept downstairs. Before their father was awake, they did every bit of work they could find to do. They even found the tailor's tape measure that had been lost for a week. Then they crept happily back to bed.

When the poor tailor came wearily downstairs, he looked around and rubbed his eyes. He looked around again and rubbed them harder. The table was set. The floor was clean. The room was bright and shiny as a new penny.

For a while, the tailor could not say a word. Then he ran to the foot of the stairs, shouting "Mother! Mary! Tommy! Our brownie has come back! And look," he said as he sat down at the table, "the brownie even found my tape measure! This is as good as a day's work to me."

One morning, the tailor woke up very early. He heard laughter coming through the floor from the kitchen below. "It must be the brownie," he thought. He put on his clothes and crept downstairs. When he opened the door to the kitchen, he saw Mary and Tommy dancing around the room.

"What's this?" he asked, when he could find his breath.

"It's the brownies," sang the children.

"The brownies? Where are they?" cried the tailor.

"Here! Here! We are the brownies!"

"But who did all the work? Where are the real brownies?"

"Here!" said Mary and Tommy as they ran into their father's arms.

When Granny heard all the noise, she came downstairs, too. The tailor told her how he had found the brownies.

"What do you think of it all, Mother?" asked the tailor.

"Children are a blessing," said the grandmother. "I told you so."

THE STORY OF GIRL SCOUTING

Girl Scouting was started in the United States in 1912 by a woman named Juliette Gordon Low. An uncle nicknamed her "Daisy" at birth. He looked at her and said, "I bet she's going to be a daisy!" And she was! Daisy was a very special person.

Daisy was born in her family's house in Savannah, Georgia, on Halloween day, October 31, 1860. She had an older sister named Nellie, two younger sisters named Alice and Mabel, and two younger brothers named Willy and Arthur.

Daisy's father was in the cotton business. Her mother was a homemaker. She took care of the family and their big house. (The house is now a national Girl Scout center. If you are ever in Savannah, Georgia, you can visit it. It's called the Birthplace and the address is 142 Bull Street, Savannah, Georgia 31401.)

◆ Look at a map of the United States. Find Savannah, Georgia. Is it far from where you live?

As a young girl, Daisy did many things. She liked to play with her brothers and sisters; take care of animals; make up stories; draw; write and be in plays; play tennis; and form clubs. She started a children's magazine that lasted five years. Children did the whole magazine by themselves.

Pretend you're working with Daisy on the children's magazine.

▲ Draw a picture for the magazine.

◆ Write a story for the magazine.

Daisy loved animals. One time she saved a kitten from being drowned in a flood. Another time she kept a cow from getting really sick by putting her mother's blanket on it overnight. Her mother was displeased in the morning because the cow had stepped on the blanket, which had fallen off. Daisy also had a horse named Fire. He was black with four white feet. She spent many hours riding, grooming, and talking to Fire. As an adult, she had a favorite parrot named Polly Poons.

▲ Draw your favorite animals, or paste pictures of some from magazines in a scrapbook.

◆ Write a story about your favorite animals.

When Daisy was older and finished with school, she married an Englishman named Willie Low. They moved to England and then to Scotland. (◆See if you can find England and Scotland on a world map.) They did not have children, but Daisy always enjoyed doing things to help young people.

Daisy's life was not always easy. She faced many troubles. She was partially deaf. Daisy also had problems in her marriage to Willie. They were not happy together. When Daisy was 45 years old, her husband died. But she did not let the troubling things in her life stop her from doing what she wanted to do. She loved to help others and had a great sense of humor. People loved to be with her because she had lots of spirit and was very friendly.

24

▲ Think about some of the troubling things that have happened in your life and how you have faced them.

Daisy heard about Girl Scouting and Boy Scouting from her friend Sir Robert Baden-Powell and his sister Agnes in England. She liked the idea of organized activities for girls.

For a while, Daisy worked with girls in Scotland. Then she returned home and started Girl Scouting in the United States. On March 12, 1912, Daisy met with the first troop of girls in Savannah, Georgia. That's why March 12 is the **Girl Scout birthday**. See page 38.

Daisy died in 1927. She was 67 years old. She had done many things in her life to make the world a better place. People around the world admire the wonderful work she did. The Juliette Low World Friendship Fund was started a few months after her death to honor Daisy and her hopes for world friendship. A ship, a United States postage stamp, and a federal government building were all named for her. A sculpture of Daisy was placed in the Georgia State Capitol.

Juliette Gordon Low had many hopes. She worked hard to make them come true. She wanted to give something special to girls—and she did. She gave us Girl Scouting!

▲ If you could do anything to make the world a better place, what would you do? Tell a friend about your ideas.

GIRL SCOUT AGE LEVELS

All girls 5 through 17 years old or in kindergarten through the twelfth grade can be members of Girl Scouting in the United States. Girl Scouting is for girls of all religions and of all colors. Every Girl Scout in the United States does the following:

- makes the Girl Scout Promise and accepts the Girl Scout Law.
- pays national membership dues to Girl Scouts of the U.S.A.
- is part of the worldwide movement of Girl Guides and Girl Scouts.

There are five age levels in Girl Scouting. They are as follows:

Daisy Girl Scout—ages 5–6 or grades K, 1

Brownie Girl Scout—ages 6, 7, 8 or grades 1, 2, 3

Junior Girl Scout—ages 8, 9, 10, 11 or grades 3, 4, 5, 6

Cadette Girl Scout—ages 11, 12, 13, 14 or grades 6, 7, 8, 9

Senior Girl Scout—ages 14, 15, 16, 17 or grades 9, 10, 11, 12

Girl Scouts usually get together with other girls in their age level to learn new things and have fun. Sometimes they come together to work on projects and to do things that help them find out about and get ready for the next age level. These activities are called **bridging**. (See page 136 for more on

Junior Girl Scout   Cadette Girl Scout   Brownie Girl Scout   Senior Girl Scout   Daisy Girl Scout

bridging.) There are even special Girl Scout ways of deciding what to do at each age level. For example, Daisy Girl Scouts form a **Daisy Girl Scout Circle** to make group decisions. They make a scrapbook and fill it with pictures, drawings, and stories of the fun things they do during the year. They receive a certificate at the beginning and end of the year.

Brownie Girl Scouts get together in the **Brownie Girl Scout Ring** to make their group decisions. They can earn **Try-Its** that are worn on their uniforms. These Try-Its show they have learned new things and had new adventures in Brownie Girl Scouting. See the chapter "Brownie Girl Scout Try-Its."

Junior Girl Scouts sometimes work in small groups called "patrols" and may hold town meetings or courts of honor to make decisions. They can earn badges, signs, and patches from their own handbook and badge book. See pages 137–141 for more things you can do when you cross the bridge to Junior Girl Scouting.

Girl Scout Gold Award

Cadette and Senior Girl Scouts make many decisions. They can earn interest project patches, leadership awards, challenges, and awards like the Girl Scout Silver Award. Like Cadette Girl Scouts, Senior Girl Scouts work on particular awards and may earn the Girl Scout Gold Award. Cadette and Senior Girl Scouts go many places, and may even travel to other states and countries.

After Senior Girl Scouting, you can become an adult in Girl Scouting. Many adults are Girl Scouts, including Girl Scout leaders. They help girls plan and carry out fun activities in Girl Scouting.

PEOPLE IN GIRL SCOUTING

You are in the center of a Girl Scout circle of friends and helpers.

▲ Fill in your name in the inside circle and read on to see who else is in the Girl Scout circle of friends.

One of the ways Girl Scouts work together is in Girl Scout troops.

▲ If you are a member of a Brownie Girl Scout troop, fill in the names of your troop friends in the next circle.

Then, to help you and the other girls, there are Girl Scout leaders.

▲ Write your leader's name in the next circle.

◆ Write in this space some things your leader does. A leader helps guide your meetings, keeps records, finds out about council events, and does many other things.

To help girls and their leaders, a number of people work together and form a Girl Scout council. Your Girl Scout council makes sure that Girl Scouting is happening where you live.

Me

My Girl Scout Friends

My Girl Scout Leader

My Girl Scout Council

Girl Scouts of the U.S.A.

World Association of Girl Guides and Girl Scouts

▲ Find out the name of your Girl Scout council and write it in the next circle.

The next circle is Girl Scouts of the U.S.A. (GSUSA, for short). GSUSA helps Girl Scout councils and individual Girl Scouts across the country. Your membership dues help to make Girl Scouting happen for girls just like you.

The last and biggest circle is for the World Association of Girl Guides and Girl Scouts (WAGGGS, for short). Your World Association pin shows that you are a part of this worldwide movement of Girl Guides and Girl Scouts. You have about eight million sisters in over one hundred countries. That's a big circle of friends!!

BROWNIE GIRL SCOUT UNIFORM

Show others how special it is to be a Brownie Girl Scout by wearing your Brownie Girl Scout uniform. This uniform tells people you are a Brownie Girl Scout.

Girl Scouts and Girl Guides from other countries have their own uniforms, too. Some of these uniforms are much like yours and others are not, as the pictures below show.

BROWNIE GIRL SCOUT INSIGNIA AND RECOGNITIONS

Girl Scout **insignia** are the pins and badges that you wear on your uniform. Some insignia, called **recognitions**, are for particular achievements. You can get Brownie Girl Scout Try-Its, a bridging patch, a Dabbler badge, and other recognitions, which are explained on the following pages. Many religious groups have their own recognitions for girls of their faith who are Girl Scouts. If you are interested in the religious recognitions, you can find out about them from your Girl Scout council or leader, or from your religious organization.

The Brownie Girl Scout pin tells others that you are a Brownie Girl Scout. It has the shape of a **trefoil**. "Trefoil" means three leaves. The leaves stand for the three parts of the Girl Scout Promise. You may wear your Brownie Girl Scout pin even when you are not wearing your uniform.

The World Association pin shows that you are a part of the World Association of Girl Guides and Girl Scouts. You may wear it on your regular clothes as well as on your uniform.

The Girl Scouts U.S.A. identification strip shows that you are part of the family of Girl Scouts in the United States of America.

The Girl Scout council strip shows the name of your local Girl Scout council.

Troop number. Every Girl Scout troop has its own number. The number is given to your troop by your Girl Scout council.

The Daisy Girl Scout pin shows that the wearer was once a Daisy Girl Scout. You do not wear this pin on your Brownie Girl Scout uniform, however. Keep it with your Daisy Girl Scout scrapbook or with other important souvenirs.

Membership star and disc. A star stands for one year of membership in Girl Scouting. You get a star for each year you are a Girl Scout. The color of the disc behind the star tells the age level you were in. The color green shows that you got the star as a Brownie Girl Scout. If you were once a Daisy Girl Scout, you will have a blue disc.

Brownie Girl Scout pin

World Association pin

Girl Scouts U.S.A. identification strip

Troop number

Girl Scout council strip

Bridging patch

Daisy Girl Scout pin

Membership star and disc

Dabbler badge

Brownie Girl Scout Try-Its

Brownie Girl Scout Try-Its. These patches, or recognitions, show your achievements in various types of activities. You get a recognition for each activity you do.

A bridging patch shows that you did particular things to help prepare you for Junior Girl Scouting. (To find out more about bridging, look at pages 135–144.)

The Dabbler badge is a recognition that you can get as part of your bridging activities. (See page 140.)

GIRL SCOUT CEREMONIES

Girl Scouts hold ceremonies for many reasons. Some ceremonies celebrate a special day in Girl Scouting. Other ceremonies are held just as a way for the group to share their feelings. Girl Scout ceremonies can be short and part of a regular meeting, or they can take up most of a meeting. They can take place indoors or outdoors.

Your Brownie Girl Scout ceremonies can include Brownie Girl Scouts, other girls in Girl Scouting, Girl Scout leaders, other adults in Girl Scouting, and special guests, like parents, guardians, relatives, and friends.

What can be done at a ceremony?

- Say the Pledge of Allegiance.
- Honor the flag.
- Say the Girl Scout Promise and Law.
- Light candles.
- Sing songs. Write and sing your own songs, too.
- Recite poems.
- Read special words and sayings.

- Tell stories.
- Act out a story.

Special Girl Scout Ceremonies

Investiture—A way to welcome someone into Girl Scouting for the first time.

Rededication—Girl Scouts who have already been invested renew their Girl Scout Promise and Law. Many girls do this at the beginning or end of the troop year.

Fly-Up—Brownie Girl Scouts become Junior Girl Scouts. This ceremony is particular to Brownie Girl Scouting.

Bridging—Girl Scouts move from one age level to another.

Court of Awards—Girl Scouts receive recognitions and insignia.

Girl Scouts' Own—A quiet ceremony designed by the troop around a theme. The girls and leaders express their feelings about the theme.

Two important ceremonies that may be used as parts of other ceremonies are the following:

Flag Ceremony—A ceremony that honors the flag of the United States.

Girl Scout Candlelight Ceremony—A candle lighting that helps remind people about the words and meaning of the Promise and Law.

Parts of a Ceremony

At the opening, everyone attending learns the reason for the ceremony. In the main part, the celebration takes place. The closing is the time to thank the guests and say good-bye.

GIRL SCOUTING'S SPECIAL DAYS

Three very big days that Girl Scouts celebrate are the following:

October 31: Juliette Low's birthday (also known as Founder's Day).

February 22: Thinking Day, the birthday of both Lord Baden-Powell and Lady Baden-Powell, the World Chief Guide.

March 12: The birthday of Girl Scouting in the United States of America.

Juliette Low's Birthday

Girl Scouts honor Juliette Low on her birthday in many different ways. These are some things you may want to do:

▲ Put on a play, skit, or puppet show about Juliette Low's life for younger girls, another troop, or invited guests.

▲ Make a picture display of Juliette Low's life or the history of Girl Scouting.

▲ Learn some Girl Scout and Girl Guide songs, and sing them at a neighborhood gathering.

▲ Invite another troop to celebrate with you and have a party.

▲ Give money to the Juliette Low World Friendship Fund. Part of this fund is used to send Girl Scouts to other countries and to bring Girl Guides to the United States. The other part is used to help Girl Scouts and Girl Guides all around the world.

Thinking Day: The Birthday of Lord and Lady Baden-Powell

Robert, Lord Baden-Powell was the founder of Boy Scouting. Olave, Lady Baden-Powell, his wife, helped Girl Scouting and Girl Guiding grow around the world. The birthday of Lord and Lady Baden-Powell has become a day for Girl Scouts and Girl Guides everywhere to "think about" each other. By doing this, you show the spirit of Girl Scouting and Girl Guiding that unites all members of the World Association in international friendship. Here are some ideas for celebrating Thinking Day:

▲ Find other Girl Scout and Girl Guide countries on a map.

▲ Make some crafts from other countries.

▲ Invite a Girl Scout who has traveled outside the United States to share her experiences with you.

▲ Make Thinking Day cards and send them to other Girl Scouts or Girl Guides you have met.

▲ Give to the Juliette Low World Friendship Fund.

▲ Hold a Girl Scouts' Own or a candlelight ceremony with each Girl Scout expressing how she feels about Thinking Day.

Girl Scout Birthday (Girl Scout Week)

Girl Scouts celebrate their own Girl Scout birthday for an entire week. The birthday is March 12, the date in 1912 when the first Girl Scout meeting in the United States was held. The week in which March 12 falls is known as Girl Scout Week.

Some of the ways you can celebrate follow:

▲ Wear your Brownie Girl Scout uniform.

▲ Hold a ceremony with other troops in the neighborhood.

▲ Set up a Girl Scout display at school or in the community. The history of Girl Scouting or Girl Scouting today is a possible subject. Can you think of others?

▲ Go to religious services on Girl Scout Sunday or Sabbath.

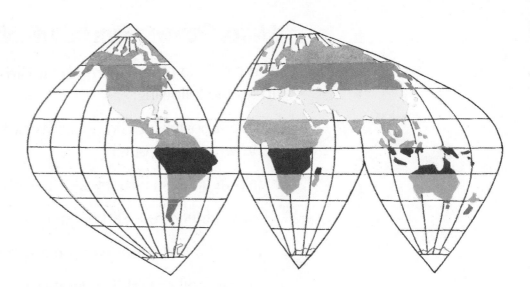

BROWNIE GIRL SCOUTS AROUND THE WORLD

A Brownie Girl Scout is a member of a worldwide family. There are Brownie Girl Scouts and Girl Guides in countries all over the world. The World Association pin, which Brownie Girl Scouts wear with the Brownie Girl Scout pin, is worn by all Girl Scouts and Girl Guides.

In India, girls in your age level are called "Bulbuls" ("Bluebirds"), and they meet in groups called "flocks." Leaders are called "Wise Birds."

In Switzerland, Brownie Girl Scouts are called "Bienli" ("Little Bees") and they meet in groups called "hives."

In Brazil, Brownie Girl Scout troops are called "cirandas." They meet in a circle or circle ring (like the Brownie Girl Scout Ring). A ciranda is a circle singing game like ring-around-the-rosy.

In Kenya, girls ages 8 through 11 are called Brownies. In the Philippines, girls ages six through nine are called Star Scouts.

▲ Look through the book *The Wide World of Girl Guiding and Girl Scouting.* Ask someone to read some of the sections with you.

▲ Talk with other Girl Scouts to learn more about Girl Guiding and Girl Scouting in other countries.

You can help others learn about Girl Scouting. You may want to do the following:

▲ Make a poster for Girl Scout Week showing things you do as a Brownie Girl Scout.

◆ Help in a flag ceremony at a neighborhood or council event.

▲ Bring a friend to a Girl Scouting event.

◆ Help get a Girl Scout camp ready for a summer season.

▲ Talk with other Girl Scouts about more ways you can let people know about Girl Scouting.

▲ Try some of the activities in the section "Girl Scout Ways," pages 157–158.

GIRL SCOUT NATIONAL CENTERS

Girl Scouts from everywhere in the United States can meet other Girl Scouts at three special places, called "national centers." Ask a leader to help you find out more about them.

The Juliette Gordon Low Girl Scout National Center is the beautiful home in Savannah, Georgia, where Juliette Low was born. People can visit this site and learn about Juliette Low's life and take part in many fun activities.

Girl Scout National Center West is in Ten Sleep, Wyoming. It includes over 14,000 acres of rugged wilderness. Visitors can learn about the West, Wyoming, wildlife, and Girl Scouting.

Edith Macy Conference Center is 35 miles north of New York City in Briarcliff Manor, New York. Many courses and conferences are given there. It is also the site of the Camp of Tomorrow, where people can learn about the out-of-doors.

WORLD CENTERS

Our Cabaña (Mexico), Our Chalet (Switzerland), Olave House (England), and Sangam (India) are four centers where older Girl Guides and Girl Scouts from all over the world can meet.

YOUR INVESTITURE OR REDEDICATION

After you have learned the Girl Scout Promise and Law, you are ready to be invested. An **investiture** is a special ceremony in which you officially become a Girl Scout for the first time. As part of the ceremony, you make the Girl Scout Promise. If you were a Daisy Girl Scout, you have already been invested and you will be rededicated as a Brownie Girl Scout. Investiture and rededication are important ceremonies in Girl Scouting. If you are being invested, you will receive your Brownie Girl Scout pin. If you are being rededicated, you may have already received your Brownie Girl Scout pin at your bridging ceremony from Daisy to Brownie Girl Scouting.

In the spaces below, fill in your name, and the date when and the place where you were invested or rededicated as a Brownie Girl Scout.

I, _____,
(your name)

was invested/rededicated as a Brownie Girl Scout on

_____ at _____.
(date)   (place)

Welcome to Brownie Girl Scouting!

41

You are very special. In this chapter, you can write or draw things that tell about you. You can write down the things you like and don't like, and the things that are important to you. There are lots of fun activities for you to try!

THIS IS ME

▲ Draw a picture or paste a photo of yourself here.

My name is _____

MY NAME

▲ Your name has a story. Find out as much as you can about your name. Ask the questions on this list or make up some of your own. Tell your name story to others.

- Who named you?
- Were you named after someone?
- Does a famous person have the same name?
- Is there a place where you live, like a street or business, that has the same name?

- How do you spell or say your name in another language? For example, Peter in French is "Pierre."

▲ Name Games. You can have fun with your name.

- Make words with the letters in your name, if possible.
- Make a design with the letters of your name.
- Make an animal or face with the letters.
- Write your name in the sand or snow, or with pebbles and rocks.
- Make a name picture. Use crayons, markers, or paint to write your name on cloth, wood, or paper. Make a frame and hang up your name on a wall or door.

MY BIRTHDAY

Your birth date is the day that you were born.

◆ Write your birth date in the cake.

▲ Draw candles on the cake to show how old you are.

▲ Draw a picture or

◆ write a story about what you did on your last birthday.

◆ Plan a birthday party. See the food Try-Its on pages 146–148 for recipes.

◆ Write an autobiography. That's a story about your life. Get a book with blank pages, or make one of your own. Include when and where you were born, your birthdays, and anything else about yourself, as when you first became a Girl Scout. Add pictures and drawings, too! Continue your autobiography as you get older.

MY BODY

▲ Your height, your weight, the size of your feet—do you know what they are? Record this information and today's date and more in the spaces. Do this once every year around the same time and see the changes in you.

FIRST YEAR

Age _____

Date today _____ 3/87 _____

Height __4__ feet and __1/2__ inches

Weight _____ pounds

Waist __18 1/2__ inches

Leg length __19 1/2__ inches

Arm length _____ 15 _____ inches

Head size __19 7/8__ inches around

Shoe size _____

Dress size _____

Blouse size _____

Pants size _____

SECOND YEAR

Age _____

Date today _____

Height _____ feet and _____ inches

Weight _____ pounds

Waist _____ inches

Leg length _____ inches

Arm length _____ inches

Head size _____ inches around

Shoe size _____

Dress size _____

Blouse size _____

Pants size _____

THIRD YEAR

Age _____

Date today _____

Height _____ feet and _____ inches

Weight _____ pounds

Waist _____ inches

Leg length _____ inches

Arm length _____ inches

Head size _____ inches around

Shoe size _____

Dress size _____

Blouse size _____

Pants size _____

45

◆ Some things about you do not change, like the color of your eyes. Write this information in the chart below.

FACTS ABOUT MY BODY

Color of eyes _____   Color of hair _____

My fingerprints. (Apply paint to your fingertips and press them on the marked spots.)

Body Tricks and Games

▲ Tape pieces of newspaper together to form a large sheet. Then lie down on your back on it. Ask someone to take a crayon or marker and trace the shape of your body onto the paper. Draw in your face and your favorite clothing to complete the picture.

▲ Try measuring things with your hands and feet. For example, how many footsteps must you take to walk across a room? to walk to school? Or find out how many hand lengths make up the length of a broomstick. Think of other things to measure.

▲ Twist and turn your fingers to make letters of the alphabet. Try using your whole body, too!

 ## MY FEELINGS

You have many feelings. Some things make you feel good inside. Some do not make you feel very good.

Things that make me happy.

▲ Draw, find pictures of, or
◆ write about things that make you happy.

Things that make me cry.

▲ Draw, find pictures of, or
◆ write about things that make you cry.

Things that scare me.

▲ Draw, find pictures of, or
◆ write about things that scare you.

Things that make me laugh.

▲ Draw, find pictures of, or

◆ write about things that make you laugh.

MY FAVORITES

You may like some things better than others.

▲ Fill in the "favorites" list. There is a space for you to write your most-liked toy, game, book, color, and more. Write the date, too. For example, one of your favorite books this year may be the *Brownie Girl Scout Handbook*. Enter the title on the line under "book" and then the date. Add to the list. You may have a favorite song or holiday, or something else that is special to you.

MY FAVORITES

toy	game	book
_____	_____	_____
_____	_____	_____
_____	_____	_____

color	school subject	sport
_____	_____	_____
_____	_____	_____

MY HOBBIES

Do you have a hobby? A hobby is a fun way to learn about new things. A hobby can be anything you really like to do when you have free time. Maybe you like to draw pictures or paint.

▲ Find pictures or draw them of things you like to do as hobbies.

◆ Write about these things.

Maybe you would like to start a hobby. Some hobbies involve making things. You could do the following:

- Make puppets (finger puppets, hand puppets, marionettes, etc.). See pages 176–179 for more ideas.
- Sew or weave things (clothes, wall hangings, pot holders, blankets, etc.). See pages 171–172 for more ideas.
- Make clay objects (bowls, cups, sculptures, etc.). See pages 170–171 for more ideas.
- Make things from wood (go-carts, walking sticks, utensils, pencil holders, etc.). See pages 130–132.

Collecting is another kind of hobby. Your collection could contain rocks, shells, coins, stickers, stamps, dolls, cards, postcards, autographs, toys, pictures, buttons, etc.

Have a safe place for your collections and keep them organized. Old shoe or cigar boxes make good collection holders. You may want to use notebooks or scrapbooks to hold some of your other collection items.

There are other hobbies involving activities. You can belong to a club; sing with a group; play a musical instrument; cook; garden; hike; read; listen to music; write letters; do sports, such as swimming, tennis, soccer, softball, or dodgeball; or watch animals.

MAKING UP MY MIND

Should I study more for my spelling test? Should I talk to the new girl in class? Should I brush my teeth this morning? You make up your mind about many things each day. You choose which book to borrow from the library or decide what to wear outside to play. When you are making up your mind about something important, think about the good and bad points. Here is a question that Vanessa, a girl like you, has asked herself. She was able to make up her mind by thinking carefully about the question.

Question: Should I wear my new jeans to soccer practice?

GOOD POINTS	BAD POINTS
1 I will look very nice.	1 The soccer field is muddy.
2 My friends will like the jeans.	2 I could fall and tear my pants at the knees.
3 My new jeans are comfortable.	3 My mother doesn't like me to wear good clothes to practice.

When Vanessa looked at the good and bad points, she decided that it would be better to wear old jeans. What do you think?

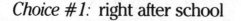 Here is a making-up-my-mind chart to help you choose the best time to do your homework. To do the chart, write down the good and bad points for each choice.

Question: When should I do my homework?

Choice #1: right after school

GOOD POINTS   BAD POINTS

1 _____   1 _____

_____   _____

2 _____   2 _____

_____   _____

3 _____   3 _____

_____   _____

Choice #2: right after dinner

GOOD POINTS   BAD POINTS

1 _____   1 _____

_____   _____

2 _____   2 _____

_____   _____

3 _____   3 _____

_____   _____

Now read over the good and bad points for each choice. Pick the time that is best for you to do your homework.

◆ Make other making-up-my-mind charts about the following: TV shows to watch; things to do after school; clothes to take to camp; spending your allowance; starting a hobby; clothes to wear to a party; books to take out from the library.

Sometimes, making a chart of the good and bad points will help you make up your mind. But even if you don't make a chart, think carefully about your choices. Making choices is something you will be doing your whole life.

WHEN I GROW UP

You may have many ideas about what you'll be like when you grow up. As you get older, your ideas about what you want in life and what you want to be may change.

▲ Draw or find pictures that show what you want to be when you grow up.

◆ Write or tell a story about yourself as a grown-up.

▲ Talk with someone who is doing what you want to do when you grow up.

There is only one you in this world. You have your own name, birthday, body, feelings, hobbies, and ideas about what you'll be like when you grow up. Because there is only one you, it's important that you know as much as you can about taking care of yourself. Read the next chapter to find out more.

TAKING CARE OF MYSELF

THE BASICS

Being good to yourself now will help you in later life. Here are some ways you can take good care of yourself:

- Exercise.
- Eat a variety of foods.
- Get a good night's sleep.
- Sit or rest quietly for a little while when you are tired.
- Dress properly for the weather.
- See your doctor and dentist for regular checkups.
- Learn to do things safely. (See pages 97–104.)
- Brush your teeth after meals and snacks.
- Bathe and comb or brush your hair regularly.

By using these health tips, you will look good and feel your best. Remember, keeping yourself healthy is up to you!

FITNESS FUN

Fitness is important for everybody. Being fit means having a strong and healthy body. Keeping fit can be easy and fun, but becoming fit does not always happen quickly. You need to exercise a little each day. Swimming, jogging, bicycling, walking, rope jumping, dancing, flying kites, skating, hiking, and other physical activities are just some ways to become and stay fit.

Find out how fit you are now. Do these exercises with an adult present until you know how to do them safely.

 Try at least two of these exercises.

- See how many sit-ups you can do in one minute. Lie on your back with your knees bent and your arms to the side. Sit up with your arms straight and palms down. Extend your hands beyond your knees. Lie back down.
- See how far you can run in 15 seconds. Ask a friend to keep time for you.
- See how far you can jump. Make or pick a starting line on the ground. Leap forward as far as you can. Measure the distance.

- See how far you can throw a ball.
- See how long you can balance on one leg. Stand on one foot, bend forward, and lift your other foot backward. Hold this position as long as you can. You may use your arms for balance.

Keep track of how you do in each exercise.
Here are some exercises you can try with your friends.

 ▲ Pretend you are different animals and try to move as they do. Divide into teams and play animal tag or animal relay.

- Rabbit jump: Bend your knees and jump forward.
- Crab walk: Sit on the floor with your hands behind you. Lift up your body with your hands and feet. Walk on all fours. Walk forward and backward in this position.
- Elephant walk: Bend forward. Extend your arms and place one hand over the other, fingers pointed toward the ground, to form a trunk. Walk slowly with legs straight and trunk swinging from side to side.

Rabbit jump

Crab walk

HERE COMES A BROWNIE!

Elephant walk

Seal crawl

Inchworm

Frog jump

54

- Seal crawl: Pull yourself forward with your hands at your side while dragging your body and feet.
- Inchworm: Place both hands on the floor. Try to keep your knees stiff and legs straight, but bend your knees if you have to. Walk forward with your hands as far as you can, and then walk forward with your feet to your hands.
- Frog jump: Squat on the floor with hands in front of feet. Jump forward and land on both hands and feet.

Make up your own animal moves and try them.

▲ Try moving your body as many ways as you can while listening to music. Walk, run, jump, skip, hop, leap, slide, gallop, bend, lift, roll, twist, and turn.

▲ Play follow-the-leader. Each person takes turns leading the group with different movements. To make it more fun, try playing this game with a hoop, rope, ball, or bean bag.

◆ Make a fitness wheel.

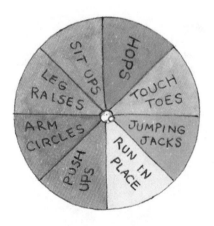

1 Cut a piece of heavy cardboard into a circle.
2 Draw four straight lines through the middle of the circle. You will have eight places to write the names of exercises. Here are some ideas:

jumping jacks	hops
running-in-place	sit-ups
toe touches	push-ups
leg raises	arm circles

3 When it's time to take a fitness break, have one girl close her eyes and point to the wheel.
4 Do the exercise that is picked for at least one minute. Do this as many times as you like. See how many exercises you can work up to.

Use the fitness wheel with music. You will need a record player, radio, or tape recorder. Start the music. Do the exercise pointed to until someone stops the music. Choose another exercise.

GAMES AND SPORTS

Playing games and sports are good ways to keep fit. Whether you play alone or with others, games and sports often have rules to follow. You should play fair and always try to do your best. When you do so, you are being a good sport. Having fun is the most important thing, not who wins or loses.

Try some of these games, in which everyone can have fun and be a winner.

▲ Ball toss. One player stands in the center, and the others form a circle around her. She tosses the ball straight up in the air and calls the name of another player. The player whose name is called runs to the center and tries to catch the ball on the first bounce. If she catches it, she becomes the new thrower. If not, the person in the center tosses again. Everyone should get a chance to be a thrower.

◆ For more excitement, try catching the ball before it bounces.

◆ Human knot. Form a close circle. Everyone reaches into the middle and joins hands with two other girls. Then, holding hands, everyone steps back a little. Try to untangle the human knot without letting go of the hands you are holding. If you can't untangle the knot, then let go and begin again.

▲ Invent your own games and play them with others.

▲ Play your favorite sport or one you would like to try with your family or friends. Swimming, bicycling, skating, and jogging are just a few activities to consider. Play fairly and safely.

◆ Make a written promise to yourself to keep fit.

The activities I plan to do to keep fit are the following:

_____

_____

_____

HEALTHY EATING

Eating healthy foods is another way of taking care of yourself. Some foods are good for you and some are not so good. You need a variety of foods to make sure that your body gets what it needs. When you eat the right kinds and amounts of food, you have a "balanced diet." Food changes into energy in your body. You need energy for everything you do. Proteins, carbohydrates (starches), fats, vitamins, minerals, and water are the nutrients in food that help your body grow and give you this energy. Foods like the following give you these nutrients:

- milk product foods such as milk and foods made from milk, like hard and soft cheese, butter, ice cream, and yogurt. For people who cannot eat milk product foods, tofu and other soy products are good substitutes.

Fruits and Vegetables

Protein Foods

Grain Foods

Milk Products

- protein foods, like meat, chicken, turkey, fish, eggs, dried beans (kidney and pinto), and nuts.
- fruits and vegetables, like oranges, apples, bananas, cherries, plantain, yucca, carrots, green beans, greens (collards, kale, spinach, and lettuce), squash, tomatoes, and fruit and vegetable juices.
- grain foods, like wheat, corn, rice, and oats. They are often dried and ground into flour, and are used to make pasta, breads, and cereals.

Eating some of these foods each day will help you to be healthy. Foods that do not have many proteins or vitamins can make you feel full without providing the things your body needs to grow. Foods like cake, candy, or potato chips have a lot of sugar, salt, or oil in them. If you eat too many of these foods, you will not stay healthy. That is why they are called junk food.

 ▲ To see if you are eating properly, keep track of all the foods you eat for one day. Fill in the chart below. Put a check mark (√) next to the kinds of foods you ate at each meal.

KINDS OF FOODS	BREAKFAST	LUNCH	DINNER	SNACKS
Milk Products	_____	_____	_____	_____
Protein Foods	_____	_____	_____	_____
Fruits and Vegetables	_____	_____	_____	_____
Grain Foods	_____	_____	_____	_____

If you have a check for all four groups for each meal, you are probably eating fairly well.

◆ Prepare your own food for a day. Find and prepare recipes that you like. Some cookbooks contain many interesting and easy-to-follow recipes. Be sure to get help from adults when trying these recipes.

◆ Play this game with two or more friends. To prepare, cut out pictures of foods from magazines and seed catalogs, and paste them on blank cards. Write the kind of food—milk, protein, fruit and vegetable, or grain—on each card to identify the food group. Ask for help if it is hard to decide. Make six or more cards for each food group. Mix up the cards and divide them evenly. Each girl picks a card from the person next to her. When you have one card from each group, put the four cards in a pile. The girl with the most piles wins.

▲ Visit a supermarket, school cafeteria, restaurant, bakery, or other place that serves or sells food. Find different foods from each group. Tell other Brownies about your trip or make something to show them about what you learned.

◆ Make a recipe file. Include recipes your family likes. Cook for your family, using someone else's favorite recipe.

Snack Time

Healthy snacks like fruits, vegetables, or milk are better for you than junk-food snacks like candy, potato chips, or soft drinks. Junk-food snacks not only lack the nutrients your body needs to grow, but they can also be a cause of tooth decay.

▲ Make a list of healthy snacks from the four food groups. Here are a few suggestions to get you started:

- peanut butter spread on apple slices
- sliced bananas rolled in chopped nuts
- fruit-juice popsicles
- carrot or celery sticks
- fresh fruit mixed with cottage cheese or yogurt
- fresh popcorn
- raisins mixed with nuts
- cheese on crackers.

59

For more food activities, see page 129 in the chapter "Things to Know."

CHOOSING YOUR CLOTHES

Why do you wear clothes? Clothing protects your body, keeping you warm when the weather is cold or cool when it is hot. Clothing can protect you from painful skin problems like windburn and sunburn.

Clothing can also show how you feel and what you like. For example, Mary loves wearing yellow because it's a bright, cheerful color.

▲ Draw a picture of your favorite outfit. What do you like about this outfit? What does it tell about you?

◆ Look at the three pictures below. What does the clothing these people are wearing tell you about them?

Wearing the right clothes will help keep you healthy and looking your best. Do you know what to wear when you go out on a cold, hot, or rainy day? Let's find out.

On cold days, wear layers of clothes. The layers hold your body heat and keep you warm. Wearing a hat is also important because a lot of body heat is lost through your head.

On hot days, loose clothing is good because it lets you move freely. Light-colored clothes are also good because they reflect the sun's rays and keep you cool.

On rainy days, you need water-repellent clothes. A raincoat, rubber boots, and an umbrella will help to keep you dry.

Dressing for the Weather Relay

 ▲ Play this game with your troop. You will need two paper bags and two sets of clothes. The clothes should be adult size and for one type of weather, which everyone can decide on.

Divide into two teams. Pick a starting and turnaround point. Have each team form a line behind the starting line. Give each team a bag of clothes.

At a signal, one girl from each team puts on the clothes in the bag. She moves as quickly as possible to the turnaround point, returns to the starting line, and takes the clothes off and puts them into the bag. She then hands the bag to the next girl in line. This continues until each girl on the team has done the same as the first girl. The first team to finish sits down and the members raise their hands.

◆ To make the game even more fun, place clothes for different kinds of weather in one bag. The team has to pick the right clothes for the kind of weather the group decides on.

See pages 116–121 for more activities on weather.

◆ Pretend you are going to these places or doing these things. Discuss what you would wear. Add your own ideas to this list:

- birthday party
- Girl Scout meeting
- shopping with your family
- riding a bicycle
- wedding
- cleaning the house
- school
- visiting a friend
- playing softball.

CARING FOR YOUR CLOTHES

Your clothes will look better and last longer if you take care of them. Hanging up your clothes, folding them neatly in your drawer, and keeping them clean are ways to make sure they will be ready when you need them and that you will look your best.

Try some of these activities:

▲ Arrange your clothes neatly in your closet or drawer.

▲ Make your own sewing kit and decorate it. Include in it thread, needles, scissors, pins, a thimble, and a tape measure.

◆ Have an adult help you learn to do at least two of the following:

- Make simple sewing repairs, like sewing on buttons and sewing up small tears.

- Handwash clothing.

- Operate a washing machine. Follow the instructions on clothes labels that tell how to care for them.

- Use and store an iron properly.

HOW YOU GROW

Your body is made up of many different parts. It does many jobs that you may not even know about. Your brain, lungs, heart, stomach, and other organs all work together to keep you healthy.

The parts of your body grow at different rates. You may also grow faster or slower than someone else your age. The most important thing is that you grow.

▲ Find baby pictures of yourself. Paste down a baby picture and one of yourself now. What changes do you see?

▲ Make a scrapbook. To show how you have grown, use photos taken of you at different ages, from your baby years to the present. See if you can find photos of you learning to walk, feeding yourself, riding a bike, and involved in other activities.

◆ Make a time line that shows how you have grown over the years. Record some of this information below on your time line.

MY TIME LINE

| Years | 0 | 1 | 2 | 3 | 4 | 5 | 6 | 7 | 8 |

- when you got your first tooth
- when you lost your first tooth
- when you said your first word
- when you first walked
- when you had your first birthday party
- when you learned to tie your shoes
- your first day at school

- when you joined your first Girl Scout troop
- when you learned to ride a tricycle
- your first visit to the dentist
- your first ride on a bus, train, or plane
- your first visit to the library
- your first trip to the zoo.

PEOPLE

Many people play a valuable part in your life. Who are they? They may be people in your family, people who are your friends, people in Girl Scouting, people in school, or people in your neighborhood.

You mean a great deal to many people in your life, too. This chapter is about you, the people in your life, and how everyone gets along together.

FAMILY

Your family includes the people who take care of you, love you, play with you, and do other things with you. They may live with you or they may live somewhere else. Some children live with their parents; some live with other people in their family. Some children have sisters and brothers; some are only children. Grandparents, cousins, aunts, uncles, and godparents are a part of families, too. Sometimes people even consider their pets as family. Who are your family members?

▲ Make a "me and my family" album. You can use words, pictures, drawings, or photographs. Here are some things to include:

- family sayings
- family get-together times
- important family dates
- favorite family meals

- favorite vacations
- traditions
- family heritage
- family talents.

 ▲ Write their names, or have them sign their names in the album below. If you have a family picture, paste it in the album to keep as a record of your family.

 ◆ Write a story or make up a song about your family. Read it or sing it for your troop.

FRIENDS

You may have friends who are important to you. Your friends are a lot like your family. Sometimes you share, play, and go places together. You may have many friends, or you may have one or two close friends. Sometimes you may work well together, sometimes you may not. You may find you like people for different reasons.

 ▲ Draw a picture and write the names of some of your friends.

It has been said that to have a friend, you must be a friend. Learning to be a friend is also an important part of Girl Scouting. Think about some of the things you can do to be a friend. Think how you can be a friend by living the Girl Scout Promise and Law.

 ◆ I am a friend when I _____

_____

_____

 ◆ I am not a friend when I _____

_____

_____

TALKING WITH PEOPLE

You can show other people how you feel in many ways—with your eyes, your hands, and even by how you stand or sit.

▲ Try to show each of these feelings without talking, and see if others can guess each one:

- sadness
- joy
- boredom
- anger

- love
- tiredness
- fear
- unsureness about something.

▲ Draw or paint pictures that express the above feelings. Your pictures may have people in them, they may be only a color, or they may have objects or patterns that bring about the feeling.

Whether you are talking with your family, friends, or people you have just met, there are ways to make sure they understand what you are saying.

1 Be a good listener. Listen to every word the person says. Decide if the person is telling you something, asking you something, or just sharing what's on her or his mind.

2 Think about what you say and how you say it. Does your voice sound angry? Do you give the other person a chance to speak? Do you treat your listener the way you would like to be treated? How would you feel if someone said to you what you are thinking of saying? Would the words make you feel happy or sad, proud or ashamed? As a Brownie Girl Scout, part of the Law you are trying to live by is "to show respect for myself and others through my words and actions."

Here are some activities to practice talking with people:

◆ Keep a diary for a day. Write how people acted when you listened carefully to what they said.

◆ Make a list of ways to show respect for others. For example:

I show respect by not making fun of what someone said.

I show respect when I listen carefully.

▲ Get a group of friends together and tape-record yourselves talking with each other while you play. How well do you talk with and listen to each other?

DECIDING WITH GIRL SCOUTS

Beyond your family and friends, you are part of another group of people—Girl Scouts. A Girl Scout learns to make decisions with other people. Brownie Girl Scouts meet in a Brownie Girl Scout Ring when they are trying to decide on something.

Group planning involves six steps. The group may not always be able to do or need to do every step, but it is important to think about all of them.

Planning and Doing Things—The Six Steps

1. Share your ideas with others.

▲ Practice sharing your ideas at Brownie Girl Scout meetings. Speak up, and let people know what you think. Try and think through what you are going to say before you say it.

▲ Play show-and-tell. Bring something from home and tell other Girl Scouts about it. This will help you feel more comfortable speaking to a group.

▲ Tell a story to a group of people. This will also help you to speak in a group.

2. Listen to others Listening to others is a very important part of planning. Practice listening by doing some of these things.

▲ Tell a group story. One person starts the story, the next person continues it, and the last person ends it.

▲ Listen to someone read or tell a story to you.

▲ Practice listening to others at Brownie Girl Scout meetings.

▲ Play telephone. One person thinks of something to say, and whispers the message to the next person, who whispers it to the next person, and so on, until the last person says the words out loud. See if the message is the same as that passed on by the first person.

3. Decide what you want to do as a group When making group decisions, remember the following:

 ▪ One person at a time should speak to the group. This helps everyone listen and pay attention.

 ▪ Everyone who wants to talk should have a chance.

 ▪ Saying something that may hurt or offend someone in the group should not be allowed.

 ▪ No one should speak too long.

 ▪ Everyone should have a say in the final decision.

Group decisions are made in many ways. Here's what one group did to start planning. Your group may not be able to or want to go through all these steps for every group decision, but this is one good way to start.

A. Each person thought about things she wanted to do and told the group. One of the Girl Scout adults made a list of each idea.

B. After checking their idea list, they made separate lists of those things they could do right away, those things they could do soon, and those things they could do much later.

C. Looking at those things they could do right away, they found out which of them people wanted to do first. They agreed to do all the things on the list, starting with the most popular and ending with the least popular.

D. They did the same thing with the list of things to do soon.

E. Next, they looked at the list of things to do later. They decided that they would be able to do all but two of the things on the list. Then they put them in the order that they wanted to do them.

F. Then they returned to the first list and made plans to start the first thing on the list.

Everyone was pleased because the group heard all the ideas and tried to be sure that everyone was satisfied. Making group decisions means give-and-take on everyone's part and is well worth the effort!

4. Make a plan Work out a step-by-step plan of what needs to be done once you have made a decision. For instance, if a group decides to have a picnic, a list of things to do and people to do them needs to be made beforehand.

A **kaper chart** is a good way to keep track of jobs. A kaper is a job. The chart shows each job and who is doing it. Look at the examples at left.

5. Carry out your plan   Have fun. Remember that things may not always turn out as you planned. Sometimes things can turn out to be more fun than you expected! Sometimes you may not have as much fun as you thought you would. Either way, it helps if you try to make every experience you have as good as it can be.

6. Think about what you've done   Was it fun? Was it a good idea? What could have made it better? Would you do it again? Then you're on to your next idea for more fun, adventure, and learning.

SCHOOL

Most Brownie Girl Scouts spend a lot of their time in school. It is a big part of your life. You can meet interesting people and learn many exciting things in school. It gives you a chance to meet many friends and do fun things together. You can work on a class project together, play in the school band, sing in the chorus, play softball, or put on a play together—and the list could go on and on and on.

My School Story

◆ Fill in the blanks below. Remember to make add-on pages as you go from year to year in Brownie Girl Scouting.

Name of my school _____

Name of my teacher _____

Name of head of my school _____

Name of my school nurse _____

Number of grades or age levels _____

Number of students _____

Number of teachers _____

Number of class pets or animals _____

Length of school day _____ hours

▲ Draw a picture of or paste a photograph of your school, or describe it in the space below.

The head of your school—sometimes called a principal or director—works with the teachers, parents, and students.

▲ Write his or her name and title.

_____

Teachers

Teachers can influence your life in many ways. What are the teachers you have met in your school life like? What do they do in the classroom?

 ▲ Use this space to write about, draw, or paste photos of some of your teachers.

People whom you will meet in school are parents, librarians, cleaning people, cooks, secretaries, guards, coaches, nurses and doctors, engineers, repair people, students, and many others.

 ▲ Make a "my school" scrapbook about some of these people. Make up stories and draw or paste pictures of them, too.

As a Brownie Girl Scout, you will continue to meet people who will play a part in your life. You may also continue to learn about what you bring to the lives of others.

My World

People, places, and things make up our world. This chapter has many interesting things for you to learn and try as you explore your home, your neighborhood, and your community. You will also learn about many countries that are part of your world.

MY HOME

Brownie Girl Scouts live in many different types of homes. For example, you may live in a two-story home, an apartment, a farmhouse, a ranchhouse, a row house, a tent, or a mobile trailer. Your home is where you live. Write your address.

▲ My address is _____ .

▲ Tell someone a story about your home.

▲ Put a drawing or photo of your home in this space.

▲ Find out how to make some things for your home by looking in the chapter "Brownie Girl Scout Try-Its" and in the section on tools on page 130 in the chapter "Things to Know."

▲ Learn how to fix things in your house.

▲ Make a crayon wall hanging.

Make crayon drawings on a plain white piece of cloth. After you have finished, ask someone to help you iron the cloth. The heat will set the crayon colors into the cloth. Follow these steps:

1 Take a sheet of aluminum foil and place it over the cloth.
2 Set the iron on low heat and press over the foil.
3 Let the cloth cool for a few minutes.
4 Then find a nice spot to hang it.

▲ Talk with the people who live with you. Find ways to help around your home. Decide what your jobs will be. Help for at least one week.

MY NEIGHBORHOOD

Your neighborhood includes the people, places, and things that are near your home. You may already have a good idea of what is in your neighborhood. Try some of these activities to get to know it even better.

▲ Take a walk around your neighborhood with someone.

▲ Help your neighbors take care of their yards or gardens, if they have them.

▲ Help welcome new children into your neighborhood.

▲ Make a scrapbook. Include drawings and photos of the people, places, and things in your neighborhood.

▲ Share something important to you with someone in your neighborhood. Find someone who would like to play with you and some of your favorite toys or games. Help someone get to know your pet, if you have one.

MY COMMUNITY

A community is made up of people living in a certain area. Your neighborhood is part of your community. You and all the other people in your community are important to each other.

Many Different People

A community may have a variety of people. Some may be very old. Some may be very young. There may be short people and tall people. There may be people who have different hair, skin, and eye colors than yours. There may be people of different religions. There may be people with disabilities. In fact, no two people in any community are exactly alike, not even identical twins. Though there are differences, we share many things and can work together to take care of our communities. Do the following to find out about your community:

▲ Look in the telephone book. Find out whether any people have the same last name as yours.

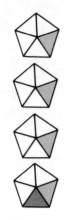 ▲ Find out where schools and houses of worship are in your community.

◆ Write a story about how your community got its name.

◆ Visit one or more of these places in your community:

- town hall
- firehouse
- voting place
- recreation department
- park
- community meeting place

- library
- hospital
- cemetery
- police station
- grange.

 ▲ Make a montage—a picture made up of many separate pictures—that tells about your community. In addition to pictures, you can also use drawings, maps, newspaper clippings, and other items.

◆ Find out the names of the newspapers in your community. Read the local news.

◆ To learn about the work people do in your community, look through the book titled *Careers to Explore for Brownie and Junior Girl Scouts,* published by Girl Scouts of the U.S.A. Try some of the activities in the book. What are some careers that you might like? Talk with people who have jobs or careers you would like to find out about.

When people work together in a community, they can help make life better for everyone. You can help to make your community a better place by being part of a service project. A service project is a task or plan for helping other people or improving your community. Service and helping are part of the Girl Scout Promise.

The following are some ways to serve your community:

 ▲ Have a pick-up-litter day around your school or Girl Scout meeting place.

▲ Remind adults to vote on voting day.

▲ Help in a community service project in your area. This may be

- a canned-goods collection for a local food pantry.
- a clothing collection project for a charitable organization.
- a collection of aluminum cans, bottles, or papers for recycling.

▲ Make brightly painted bedside litter bags for hospital patients.

 ◆ Visit people who are unable to get out into the community because of a disability, old age, or illness. Put on plays or sing songs for them.

◆ Adopt a grandparent. Do errands and visit during the week.

79

◆ Visit nursery schools and day-care centers. Show other children how to play games you know, and teach them how to make things.

◆ Help a playground assistant.

As you explore your community, you are going to meet many people. Some of the people you meet may have a disability. You may have a disability yourself. A disability is something that may make it harder for a person to do certain things.

There are many different types of disabilities. For example, a person who is blind cannot see. The person has to learn to "see" by using other senses, like hearing and touch. A person who is deaf cannot hear but will use other ways, like lip-reading, to find out about her or his world. Some people with disabilities may need wheelchairs to get around. Another person may have a learning disability.

Remember that people are people no matter how they may look, act, walk, or talk. Everyone has feelings. Staring at, laughing at, or making fun of people with disabilities may make them feel hurt, embarrassed, or angry.

Try some of these activities to understand more about disabilities.

Blind Walk

▲ Feel what it's like to be unable to see. Have a partner blindfold you and walk around with you slowly to make sure you don't get hurt. Stop to feel things. Use your senses of touch, hearing, and smell to learn about your environment.

Learn a New Language

People who cannot hear often learn how to use sign language. There are different systems of sign language.

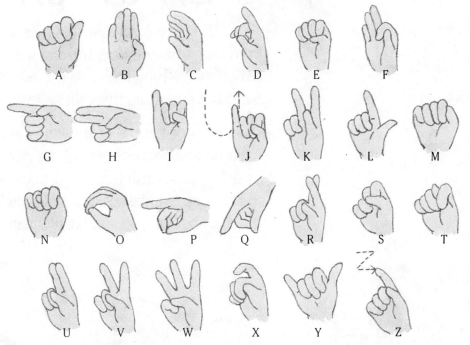

 ◆ Use the sign alphabet chart to figure out the message below. Each hand position stands for a letter.

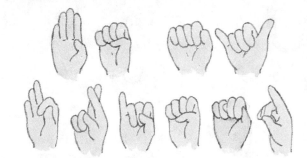

 ◆ Practice making words with this new alphabet. If you meet someone who cannot hear, you'll be able to "talk" with her or him if she or he knows this alphabet.

Mirror Image

Some people have trouble learning how to read. Letters may look mixed up to them. It's hard for them to make sense out of words on the page. This condition is called "dyslexia" (dis-lek-see-uh).

▲ To see what this disability is like, try to read the message below.

THIS IS HARD TO READ

To figure out what this message says, hold the page up to a mirror. Imagine how it must feel to have to learn to read when everything looks so mixed up! However, most people who have reading disabilities eventually do learn how to read.

◆ Learn about some of the supports for people with various disabilities: helmets, wheelchairs, seeing-eye dogs, braille, hearing aids, crutches, leg braces, walkers, canes, tape recorders, eyeglasses, reading machines, computers, talking books, special telephones, artificial limbs, special televisions.

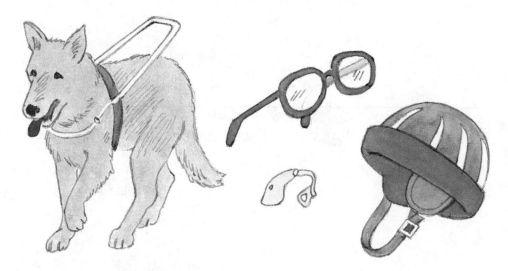

▲ Visit a school, center, home, hospital, or other site that serves people with disabilities. Learn as much as you can about what people do there.

MY NATURAL ENVIRONMENT

Your world is more than people and buildings. The air, land, water, plants, and animals are part of your world. They are part of your natural environment. You can help make the environment better for you and all the other living things you share it with. Try some of the activities below to learn more about your environment.

Adopt a Tree

▲ Adopt a tree and learn as much as you can about it. Look at it. Touch it. Find out what kind of tree it is by studying its trunk and leaves or needles and then trying to find the same kind of tree in a guide to trees. Your library may have such a book. Watch how the tree changes through the year. Do animals live in it or use it in some way?

Mini-Environment Study

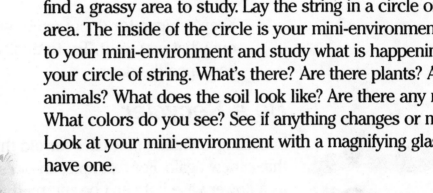

▲ Get a piece of string about two feet long. Go outdoors and find a grassy area to study. Lay the string in a circle on the area. The inside of the circle is your mini-environment. Sit next to your mini-environment and study what is happening inside your circle of string. What's there? Are there plants? Are there animals? What does the soil look like? Are there any rocks? What colors do you see? See if anything changes or moves. Look at your mini-environment with a magnifying glass, if you have one.

▲ Do some of the Try-Its activities in the World of the Out-of-Doors Try-Its and on pages 122–129 in the chapter "Things to Know."

You may know the word "pollution." Pollution is waste that spoils the environment. Among the many kinds of pollution are air pollution, water pollution, and noise pollution. You can help prevent pollution by not littering. Think of some other ways to fight pollution.

Be a Water and Energy Saver

The clean water that we use for everyday purposes, like bathing and washing the dishes, is in limited supply. To ensure that we do not use up our water reserves, we must avoid waste. The same is true for electricity and other forms of energy.

▲ Save water and electricity by practicing the following and by reminding your family to do the same:

- Do not let the water run while brushing your teeth.

- Do not let the water run while scraping and soaping the dishes.

- Fill only half the tub when taking a bath.

- Turn off the radio and television when nobody is using them.

- Turn off unnecessary lights.

- Turn off air conditioners and fans when they are not needed.

- Keep refrigerator doors open only long enough to get out what you want. Try to think of what you want before you open the door.

Be a Recycler

Recycling is finding new uses for old things or making old things new again. For example, an old soda bottle can be used as a flower vase if it can't be returned to a store. An old tire can be attached to a tree limb by a chain and used as a swing. An old inner tube makes a good swimming float.

More communities in the United States of America are learning how to recycle things. Recycling is one way to have less garbage. Glass and plastic bottles, aluminum cans, newspapers, metal from old cars, clothing, and many other things can be recycled.

Homemade Recycled Paper

◆ A fun recycling activity is making your own paper. As you get good at this, you can make paper for books, posters, newsletters, paintings, and many other things.
You will need the following supplies:

mixing bowl (large)	screen about three inches
eggbeater	square or bigger
cup	flat pan a little larger
big spoon	than the screen
old newspaper	starch.
water	

Directions:

1 Tear up half a page of newspaper in very small pieces. Put the paper in a large mixing bowl full of water.

2 Let the paper soak for one hour.

3 Beat the paper with an eggbeater for 10 minutes. The paper should be soft and mushy. It is now called "pulp."

4 Mix two tablespoons of starch in one cup of water. Add this to the pulp. Stir well. The starch makes the paper pulp strong.

5 Pour the pulp into the flat pan.

6 Place the screen in the bottom of the pan. It will become evenly covered with pulp.

7 Put the rest of the newspaper on a table. Place the screen covered with pulp on one half of the newspaper.

blotter

8 Fold the other half of the newspaper over the top of the screen. Press down very hard.

9 Fold back the newspaper so you can see the pulp. Let it dry overnight.

10 When it is dry, peel your recycled paper from the screen.

MY COUNTRY AND MY WORLD

Beyond your family, neighborhood, and community, you are also part of a country and the world. People may look different, eat and dress differently, have different holidays, live in different types of shelters, and speak different languages. All these differences make living in this world interesting and exciting. Imagine how boring the world would be if everyone and everything was the same! But people in your country and all over the world need the same basic things, like food, clothing, shelter, and love. All people need a language to communicate with others in, money, and transportation. Can you think of other things everyone needs?

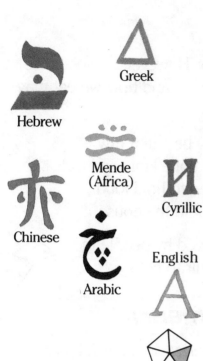

Hebrew

Greek

Mende
(Africa)

Chinese

Cyrillic

Arabic

English

There is no one "right" way to live, look, talk, dress, eat, or act. For example, a girl from Tibet may learn to stick out her tongue to show courtesy to others. In the United States of America, this gesture shows disrespect and is a way to tease someone. In India, one way to say "yes" is to shake your head back and forth from left to right. In the United States of America, this means "no!"

The activities that follow will help you learn more about people in your country and the world.

If you were to travel around the world, you would see people dressed in various ways. Climate and available materials are two reasons clothing may differ from country to country and from one continent to another.

 ▲ Find out about the kinds of clothing in other countries by reading illustrated books on the subject. If possible, invite someone to show you and your friends some examples of clothing from other countries.

▲ Find out about the differences in Brownie Girl Scout uniforms around the world. See page 39 for more about Girl Scouting around the world.

There are also different names for money in most countries around the world. You may know about dollars and cents, but children in France know about francs and centimes.

▲ See if you can find out more. Pages 112–116 are one place to start.

COUNTRY	MONEY	COUNTRY	MONEY
Albania	lek	Iraq	dinar
China	yuan	Ireland	pound
Ecuador	sucre	Japan	yen
Ethiopia	dollar	Mexico	peso
Hong Kong	dollar	Sweden	krona
India	rupee	West Germany	deutsche mark

International Food

Everyone needs food to live and grow. However, the foods we eat, the ways we prepare and cook them, and how we eat may differ. For example, in some countries

- some things that you cook may be eaten raw.
- chopsticks may be used instead of a knife and fork.
- a bowl, not a plate, may be used to hold food.
- ovens may be outdoors and not in the house.

 Try finding and making recipes enjoyed by people in various parts of the world. Ask an adult to help you.

The United States of America

Your country, the United States of America, is special. It is a country of people who come from all parts of the world and bring their individual ways with them. The United States is like a mosaic or puzzle made up of many different pieces.

 ▲ **UNITED STATES OF AMERICA MONTAGE.** To make a montage of the United States of America, you will need to find pictures and drawings that show the different parts of the country. Look for mountains, forests, lakes, rivers, and deserts. Also look for pictures and drawings that show the many people who live in the United States.

Add your own drawings and words to show how we all live in the United States of America. You will also need poster paper, scissors, and glue.

1 Decide where to put the pictures on the poster.
2 Glue everything in place.
3 Show your montage to your friends.

More to do: Work with your friends to put together a big United States of America montage.

Games around the World

Children around the world have their own games and ways to play. Try some of these games from different parts of the world.

You may find that you have your own version of some of the games. Try other games in the Try-Its section "Play" on page 155.

▲ **RABBIT WITHOUT A HOUSE (Brazil).** This Brazilian game is best when you have at least 11 people.

1 Pick someone to be "it" (the rabbit without a house) and someone to be the caller.
2 Divide the others into groups of three.
3 Each group makes a rabbit in a house by two girls holding hands (the house) and one girl (a rabbit) standing inside.
4 The caller yells out "Find a house" and all the rabbits, including the one without a house, have to run to find another house.
5 The rabbit left without a house becomes it.

▲ **JAN-KEN-PON (Japan).** You'll need two players.

1 Two players face each other with their hands behind them.
2 Together, they say "jan-ken-pon." On "pon," both bring a hand forward to stand for a stone (a fist), paper (flat hand), or scissors (V-shape with the index and middle finger).
3 Stone beats scissors because it can break them. Scissors beat paper because they can cut it. Paper beats stone because it can wrap up the stone.
4 A player gets a point each time her hand beats the other's. The first player who gets seven points wins.

▲ **MR. BEAR (Sweden).** You'll need at least three people, a place for "home," and the bear's den.

1 One person is Mr. Bear. He is trying to sleep in his den.
2 The other players sneak up to Mr. Bear and whisper "Mr. Bear, are you awake?"
3 Mr. Bear pretends not to hear them. Then the players yell, "MR. BEAR, ARE YOU AWAKE?" This makes Mr. Bear furious! He chases them all and tries to catch them before they reach home, which is the safe place.
4 Everyone tagged by the bear before reaching home becomes Mr. Bear's cubs. They go back to the den with Mr. Bear.

5 When the remaining players come back to wake up Mr. Bear again, the cubs help Mr. Bear catch them.

6 When everyone has been caught, Mr. Bear picks someone else to take his place.

 ▲ **HAWK AND HENS (Zimbabwe).** You'll need at least four people and two safety zones.

1 One person is the hawk.

2 All the other players are hens.

3 The hawk stands between the safety zones and tries to catch the hens as they run back and forth from one safety zone to the other.

4 When a hen is caught, she sits on the side and watches the game.

5 The last hen to be caught by the hawk becomes the next hawk.

Songs from around the World

Many songs from around the world are printed in *Sing Together*, published by Girl Scouts of the U.S.A., and in *Canciones de Nuestra Cabaña (Songs of Our Cabaña),* published by the World Association of Girl Guides and Girl Scouts. Four of them are reprinted here.

Merci, Seigneur

France

Mer - ci, Seig - neur,   Mer - ci, Seig - neur,   Mer - ci, Seig - neur.

Gracias à Dios.   Thank you, God.

From *Canciones de Nuestra Cabaña*, page 61. Copyright 1980 by the World Association of Girl Guides and Girl Scouts.

Kum Ba Ya

Slowly, with dignity

African

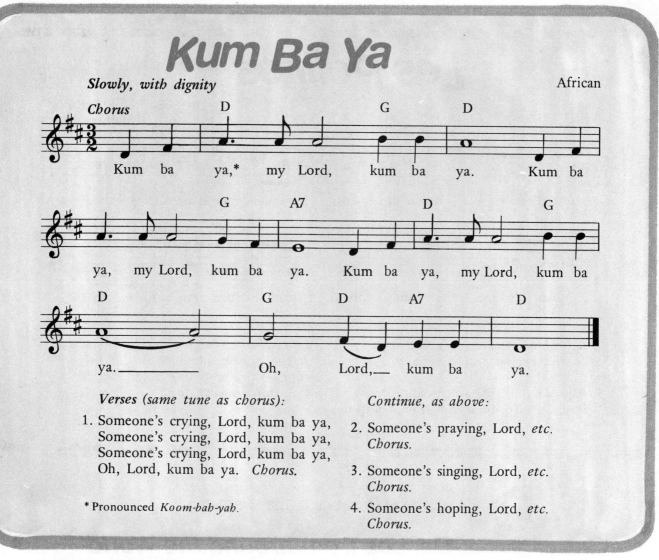

Kum ba ya,* my Lord, kum ba ya. Kum ba
ya, my Lord, kum ba ya. Kum ba ya, my Lord, kum ba
ya._____ Oh, Lord,__ kum ba ya.

Verses (same tune as chorus):

1. Someone's crying, Lord, kum ba ya,
   Someone's crying, Lord, kum ba ya,
   Someone's crying, Lord, kum ba ya,
   Oh, Lord, kum ba ya. *Chorus.*

* Pronounced *Koom-bah-yah.*

Continue, as above:

2. Someone's praying, Lord, *etc.*
   Chorus.

3. Someone's singing, Lord, *etc.*
   Chorus.

4. Someone's hoping, Lord, *etc.*
   Chorus.

Words and music by Marvin V. Frey, with African
(Angolan) translation. Copyright 1957, 1977, 1985. All
rights reserved. Used by permission.

For Health and Strength

Marcato

England

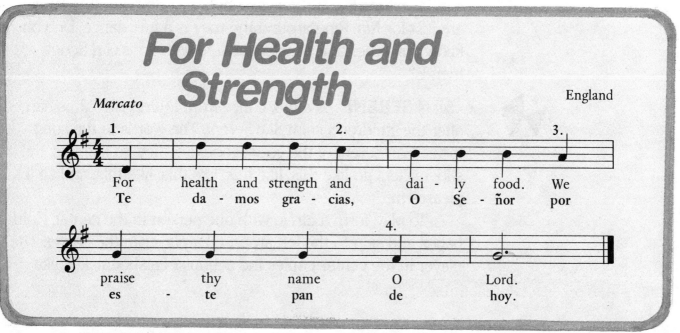

For health and strength and dai - ly food. We
Te da - mos gra - cias, O Se - ñor por

praise thy name O Lord.
es - te name pan de hoy.

Los Pollitos

Guayaquil, Ecuador
Traditional

1. Los po - lli - tos di - cen, "Pí - o, pí - o, pí - o."

Cuan - do tien - en ham - bre, cuan - do tien - en frí - o.

2. La gallina busca el maíz y el trigo
   para su comida, y les presta abrigo.

3. Bajo sus dos alas, acurrucaditos.
   Hasta el otro día duermen los pollitos.

Little chicks say "pio, pio" when they are hungry or cold. The hen looks for corn, and beneath her wings the chicks sleep till the next day.

 ▲ Learn at least one of the songs.

Dances from around the World

All over the world, people have made up folk dances and singing games. Some of the dances are used to celebrate special events like birthdays or holidays. Some of the dances are just for fun. Ring-around-the-rosy is a folk dance. Do you know any other folk dances to share with your Girl Scout friends?

 ▲ **SAN SERENI** is a folk dance from Puerto Rico. It is named after the children's saint San Sereni. The words in the song mean "San Sereni of the good, good life, they go like this, the shoemakers go like this, like this, like this, like this, and so it pleases me."

To play, form a circle with one person in the center. Hold hands and skip to the left around the player in the center. The player in the center copies the actions of a shoemaker, like driving nails into the heel of a shoe with a hammer. After the word "zapateros" (shoemakers), the players in the circle stand still and copy the actions of the center player on the words "asi, asi, asi, asi."

Each time you sing the song, another player goes in the center. Here are other jobs to act out: los carpinteros (carpenters), las lavanderas (washerwomen), las planchadoras (ironers), las campaneras (bellringers), las costureras (dressmakers), los jardineros (gardeners), los barqueros (boatmen), etc.

San Sereni

Puerto Rico
Singing Game

San Se - re - ní de la bue - na, bue - na vi - da,

ha - cen a - sí, a - sí los za - pa - te - ros, a -

sí, a - sí, a - sí, a - sí me gus - ta a mí.

◆ **LUMMI STICKS**.   Learn to play and dance to the beat of lummi sticks. Some people believe that these sticks were first used by the Lummi tribe in what is now the state of Washington, but no one knows for sure. A dance similar to the following is also popular among the Maori people in New Zealand and Filipinos.

You'll need two broomsticks or rods about 15 inches in length for each person.

1 Each person gets two sticks and finds a partner. Partners sit on the floor facing each other with legs crossed and hold a stick in each hand.

2 Everyone hits the sticks on the floor and against their partners' sticks. They can also tap sticks to the right or to the left.

3 Play with the lummi sticks until everyone is on the same beat.

4 While half the group play with lummi sticks, the other half dance to the beat. Take turns playing with the sticks and dancing.

◆ More to try:
Play lummi sticks to the beat of music while other girls dance.

Your world can be as large as the whole earth and include its three billion people. Your world can also be as small as a tiny violet growing in a park. You are a special part of the world. You can make things, and find out things, and help make the world a better place. If you could do anything, how would you change the world?

◆ Write here some of the wishes you have for the world.

_____

_____

_____

_____

_____

_____

_____

Remember
you may be able to help them come true!

THINGS TO KNOW

As you live from day to day, you learn more and more. This chapter has sections on safety, first aid, time, money, weather, outdoor skills, and being on your own. It contains information you need to know for your own well-being.

SAFETY

Dear Brownie Girl Scouts,

Being safe is more than crossing the street when the light is green. It's more than learning how to ride a bike. This part will teach you the following important safety tips:

Safety is everybody's job.
Take time to learn safety rules.
Always let an adult know what you're doing.
You can take care of yourself.

Stay with your buddy or group. Don't wander off alone.
Act safely all the time.
Find out about safety.
Enjoy being safe.

I'll continue to see you throughout the book!

Sincerely,

Suzy Safety

What does it mean to be safe? You are safe when there is nothing to harm you. What are some things that can harm you? Can you add to this list?

fires   muggers
bad drivers   home hazards
some strangers   pollution

What can you do to stay safe?

 ◆ You can be ready for emergencies. Ask a parent or guardian to help you make a list of numbers to keep by the telephone.

Emergency Who's Who

EMERGENCY WHO'S WHO

Mom at work _____

Dad at work _____

Guardian at work _____

Other relative _____

Neighbor _____

Dentist _____

Police _____

Ambulance _____

Doctor _____

Medical emergency team _____

Fire department _____

Health department _____

Poison control center _____

Air pollution control _____

What would you say or do if you had to make an emergency call? Follow the emergency guide below:

1 Use the emergency who's who list and dial the number you need.

2 Tell who you are. "Hello, my name is _____."

3 Tell where you are. "I am at _____."
(street, apt. number, city, state)

4 Tell what the emergency is. "This is an emergency.
I need _____."

Stay calm and follow directions.

Personal Safety

This section contains some do's and don'ts for Brownie Girl Scouts.

If a stranger tries to talk to you from a car, remember the following:

DON'T go near the car, even if the person said your mother told him or her to pick you up. Get away!

While walking, follow these guidelines:

DON'T take shortcuts through dark alleys, deserted buildings, or parks after dark.

DO walk with a friend.

If approached by a stranger while at school or a troop meeting, remember the following:

DON'T get into a conversation with him or her.

DO send him or her to a teacher, office, or troop leader if you are asked for directions.

DON'T believe any message he or she gives you.

DON'T take any candy, gum, or other gifts from a stranger.

DON'T enter any buildings or rooms with strangers.

DON'T play on elevators.

At home, follow these tips:

DO hang up if a stranger asks you questions on the phone.

DON'T tell a stranger you are home alone.

DON'T open the door to a stranger.

DO call an emergency number if something makes you suspicious or frightened.

In play areas, follow these guidelines:

DO play where you can be seen by the person taking care of you.

DON'T play in deserted or out-of-the-way places, such as abandoned buildings, empty laundry rooms, or storerooms.

DON'T leave the school grounds during a break or recess.

DON'T play around construction sites or mining sites.

While waiting for public transportation, remember the following:

DO find a well-lighted and busy transit stop.

If someone comes up to you whom you think intends to harm you, RUN FOR HELP.

On public transportation, do the following:

DO sit near the conductor or driver, a couple, or a family.

DO ask a conductor or driver on a bus or subway to help you if you are worried that someone may harm you.

DO change seats if someone near you makes you worried.

When using public restrooms, remember the following:

DO take someone with you.

DON'T talk to strangers or let them touch you.

Do try to remember the following if you see something suspicious or if a stranger approaches you offering a ride or a treat. It is the type of information most often needed by the police. What happened? When did it happen? Where did it happen? Try to remember some things about the car, truck, or van, such as the number of people in it, and the color, make, model, and license plate number. If you have a pen or pencil and paper, write down this information.

Try to remember what the people looked like. Think of such things as sex, height, weight, hair color and cut, eye color and whether they wore glasses, and complexion. Did they have beards, moustaches, or sideburns? How did they talk? What were they wearing?

Remember the following:

Never get into a car with a stranger.
Never let a stranger touch you.
Never believe a stranger until you have checked his or her information with someone else.
Never give information to a stranger over the phone.
Never open the door to a stranger.
Never tell a stranger you are alone.

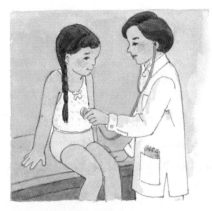

Safety with People

Lots of people touch you. For example, your parents hug you. Your brothers and sisters and you touch when you play. Your baby-sitter helps you get ready for bed. Doctors and dentists touch you when you go for checkups. But don't let a stranger touch you. If a stranger tries to touch or attack you, run to the nearest person you can find.

If someone's touch makes you feel uneasy or scared, you have the right to say "No!" even if you know the person. Inform a parent or another adult. It is very important to let someone know.

This neighbor invites you inside his house for cookies.
You don't feel comfortable.
You say "No" and leave.
You can say "No" to adults.
You should not do something that makes you feel "funny."

▲ Color in only the spaces that contain dots. Read the message.

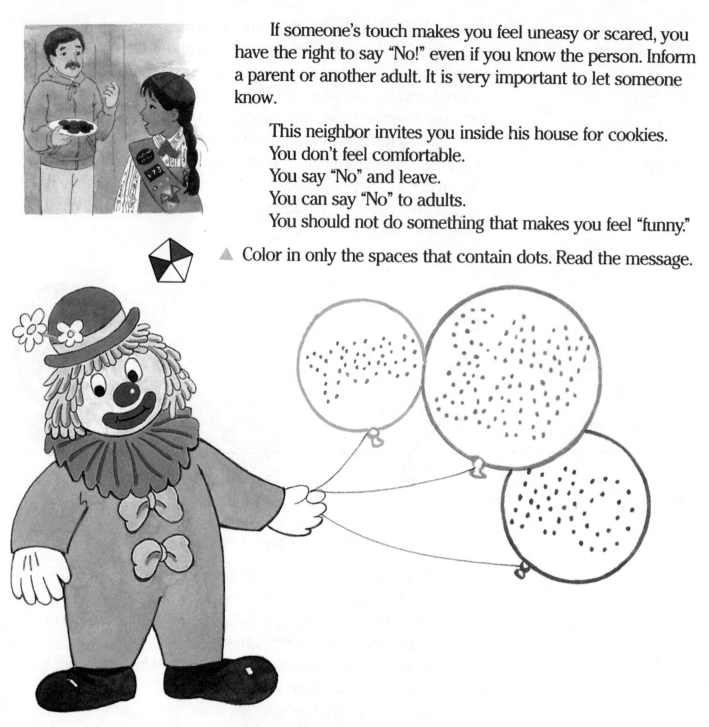

Fire Safety

With your family, prepare a what-to-do-in-case-of-fire plan. The first part of the plan should be making your home as safe as possible. Most fires can be prevented. Look for fire hazards. A fire hazard is anything that can cause a fire indoors or outdoors. Make a checklist of things to do to reduce the danger of fire. The second part should be a home fire drill.

102

Know the best way to get out of your home, especially from the bedrooms.

▲ Smoke detectors can help make your home safer. Find out about smoke detectors.

Can you spot the fire dangers in this picture?
Check your answers
with your leader.

If your clothes catch on fire, do the following:

1 STOP. Do not run or walk or jump around. Moving around adds more oxygen to the fire and keeps it going.

2 DROP. Drop to the ground or floor. Cover your face with your hands.

3 ROLL. Smother the fire by rolling over slowly.

If another person's clothes catch on fire, do the following:

1 Get the person to the ground.

2 Roll her or him over, or use a coat or blanket to smother the flames.

3 Be careful that your own clothing does not catch fire.

Your Community Health and Safety Workers

Many people have careers involving the health and safety of others. Get to know who they are and what their jobs are like.

◆ Activity—Each scrambled word matches one of the jobs (but not the job across from it). Unscramble the word and match it to the right job. The answers follow the activity.

1 Who makes sure that people obey traffic laws?

gdo ccahetr

_____

2 Who puts out fires?

ehoteepln
reptaoro

_____

3 Who gives you health checkups and vaccinations?

coliep

_____

4 Who gives you the correct telephone number?

bamanlecu vidrer

_____

5 Who collects garbage and trash and cleans the streets?

erfi fghitre

_____

6 Who keeps stray animals from running loose?

tnidtse

_____

7 Who checks to see that your teeth and gums are healthy?

codrot

_____

8 Who will drive you to the hospital in an emergency?

nstiaonait krorwe

_____

Answers: dogcatcher, telephone operator, police, ambulance driver, fire fighter, dentist, doctor, sanitation worker.

▲ Name other community workers who help keep us safe and healthy. Pick one of the workers whom you named above to learn more about. With a partner, interview this worker or have her or him visit your troop. Think about the questions before the interview. For information, who, what, when, where, why, and how questions are best. Tell others what you find out, or write a news story about the interview.

FIRST AID

First aid is the first help an injured or sick person receives. First aid may be washing a cut, putting on a Band-Aid, saying helpful things, or sending for a doctor if the situation requires one.

First-Aid Kit

▲ You can be a first aider by making first-aid kits for use at home, in the car, and at Girl Scout outings.

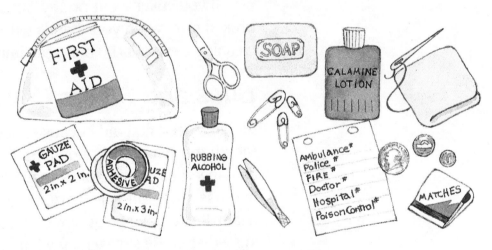

Here are some things to put in the kit:
- first-aid book
- soap
- safety pins
- scissors
- calamine lotion in an unbreakable container
- tweezer
- sewing needle
- matches

- adhesive tape and sterile gauze dressings
- rubbing alcohol in an unbreakable bottle
- clean cloth
- emergency telephone numbers, including those of a doctor, hospital, ambulance service, police, fire department, poison control center
- money for phone calls.

Infections

A simple injury can become dangerous if infection sets in. An infection is the growth of bacteria, or germs, in your body, and occurs if a wound is not taken care of properly. Signs of infection include the following:

- swelling
- redness
- a hot feeling
- pain
- tenderness
- fever
- pus.

If you suffer a cut or any other injury that results in broken skin, wash your hands with soap and water before cleaning the wound. Then seek immediate medical care.

Bites and Stings

All bites need first aid because bacteria and germs in the mouth may cause infection and disease. Even small bites can be dangerous. Animal bites may be particularly dangerous because some animals carry rabies, a disease that can cause death. If you have been bitten by an animal, tell an adult immediately. Be sure to say what kind of animal bit you.

You may need to give first aid to yourself, if no one is nearby. If so, follow these steps:

1 Wash your hands with soap and water.
2 Wash the wound with soap and water.
3 Rinse the wound well with clear water.
4 Blot the wound dry with a clean towel.
5 Apply a bandage.
6 See a doctor.

Most insect bites, like those by a mosquito, are not serious, though they do cause your skin to itch and swell up. A bee sting is often painful, but should not be a cause for real concern for most people, either. If you are stung by a bee, and its stinger remains in your skin, try to scrape it out with your fingernail. Don't squeeze the stinger, as doing so will force the poison into your body. Press a cold washcloth or ice cube against the area where you were stung.

Some people do have allergic reactions when stung by bees. They may develop trouble breathing and be affected in other life-threatening ways. Such people need fast medical attention, and should be rushed to a doctor or the hospital.

Burns

A burn is an injury to your skin from heat or chemicals.

If you have a burn, run cold water, not ice water, over the burned area. Be gentle with your skin, and don't break blisters that may form. Protect the burned area with clean cloth bandages. Find an adult to help you take care of the burn and to decide whether you need to see a doctor or go to the hospital.

Too Much Body Heat

Your body can overheat. Heat exhaustion comes from staying in hot or sunny weather too long. Signs of heat exhaustion are dizziness, cramps, headache, or a slight fever. Get out of the sun and tell an adult you don't feel well. Ask her or him to take care of you by cooling you off with water and having you drink cool water. To help prevent heat exhaustion, protect the top of your head with a hat. Even with a hat, be careful on hot days.

Too Little Body Heat

Your body can get too cold. Dangerously low body temperature is called "hypothermia" (hi-po-ther-me-ah). It doesn't have to be freezing or snowing for your body temperature to get too low. This condition can result from being out too long in cold or windy weather, or from staying out too long when it is wet or damp. If you start to shiver and your teeth chatter, you should go inside quickly and eat or drink something warm.

Frostbite

In very low temperatures, parts of your body that are not protected may actually start to freeze. This is "frostbite." Most frostbite starts on the nose, cheeks, ears, toes, and fingers, especially if they are not covered well. Signs of frostbite are the following:

1 Skin turns white or grayish-yellow.
2 Pain is no longer felt.
3 Blisters appear.
4 Skin feels cold and numb.

Frostbite is very dangerous. In any case of frostbite, it is important to do the following:

1 Go indoors and warm up. Don't rub the frostbite.
2 Find an adult to help you.
3 See a doctor as soon as possible.

Nosebleeds

Nosebleeds may follow a cold or occur after too much exercise. They may result from being in very high places, like the mountains, or from injury to the nose. They are usually not serious, but you should try to stop the bleeding. If you do get a nosebleed, sit down and squeeze your nose firmly for about 10 minutes. Placing cold towels on your nose may help. If the bleeding continues, have an adult assist you.

TIME

Time can be measured in years, months, days, hours, minutes, or seconds. As time goes by, most things change—including you. In what ways are you different today from this time last year? two years ago? when you were a baby?

▲ Find out how time changes these things:

- dead insect
- rock
- leaf
- newspaper
- cup of water with a nail in it
- chunk of potato or carrot

Put these things next to each other in a place where they can be left alone. Check on them once a week for about two months. Do you notice any changes? What has happened?

Telling Time

Time is important to most people. Look at all the clocks around you and all the people who wear watches. Do you wear a watch? Do your friends?

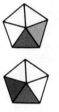 ▲ Ask people why they wear watches.

▲ Cut out or draw pictures of different kinds of clocks and watches. Paste them here.

▲ Have a clock hunt with your troop. Find as many places as you can where there are clocks.

▲ Fill in this box to show the times that you do different things. If you don't know the times, ask someone to help you.

MY TIME BOX

Time I wake up for school _____

Time school starts _____

Time I eat dinner _____

Time I go to bed on school nights _____

Time I go to bed on weekends _____

Time my Brownie Girl Scout meeting begins _____

Time my Brownie Girl Scout meeting ends _____

MONEY

You can find out lots of things by looking carefully at money. Ask your leader or parents to let you look at a one-dollar bill, a five-dollar bill, a penny, a nickel, a dime, and a quarter.

 ▲ Draw pictures of different paper bills and coins.

▲ Cover a coin with a plain white sheet of paper. Rub a crayon or pencil over the paper and the coin's design will form.

◆ What can you find on all bills and coins? Your list may start with dates and faces. What else can you find?

_____

_____

_____

_____

 ◆ Who are the people on the bills and coins? What are they famous for?

Using Money

We pay money for food and clothing. We also pay money to people who do helpful acts, such as a piano teacher for lessons and a doctor for treating us when we are sick.

When you spend money for an item, you are being a consumer. Consumers make decisions about buying.

If you get an allowance, how much do you get? How often? How do you use it? Do you save any of it?

You may also get money on certain occasions, like a holiday. Have you ever received money as a gift? What did you do with it? Sometimes your parents or another family member may give you money because you need something. Maybe you want to buy a card or gift for a friend's birthday.

▲ The next time someone in your family goes shopping, ask to go along. Ask these questions:

- Why buy one brand rather than another?
- Why buy one size rather than another?
- Why do some people use coupons? Where do you get them? How do they work?

Troop Money

The troop gets money for activities through troop dues and money-earning projects. Troop dues are used to help you and your friends do things you want to do. But for some activities, like camping trips, your troop may need to earn extra money.

These are some money-earning ideas:

- selling home-grown plants
- washing cars
- having a garage sale (your friends and family can donate things)
- selling lemonade
- having a bake sale.

Your leader can help you put your ideas into action. She can also help your troop come up with other ideas. You should be able to make money and have fun at the same time!

One way for Girl Scout troops to earn money is by selling Girl Scout cookies. If you have a sale of Girl Scout cookies or other Girl Scout products, do the following:

- Learn the good points about the Girl Scout cookies or other Girl Scout products you are selling. Be able to talk to customers about the products.
- Find out who will earn money from the sale.
- Decide how much you think you can earn.
- Plan what to do with your earnings.

▲ Let's say your troop decides to go to the zoo. What will you need to spend money on? Think about how you will get there. Will there be a bus ride to pay for? Will you buy food to feed the animals, if zoo regulations permit you to do so? What else may you buy on your trip? Discuss the outing at a troop meeting.

Checks and Credit Cards

People often use cash—bills and coins—to buy things. Sometimes people write out checks. If you buy a toaster at a hardware store, for example, and pay for it with a check, the amount of the check is subtracted from the money you have in your checking account at the bank. And sometimes people use plastic credit cards to charge their purchases. The credit card company sends a bill for all purchases once a month. In this way, you don't need to have cash with you in order to buy an item.

◆ Visit stores to find out which ones accept checks or credit cards. Look for signs in the stores that state if credit cards may be used, and which ones. Ask store owners or workers why they allow customers to use credit cards or checks.

 ▲ Have you ever seen anyone in your family pay for an item with a check or credit card? Ask why that form of money was used.

▲ Collect newspaper advertisements or fliers for stores. Do they tell you whether the stores accept credit cards or checks?

Bartering

People don't always use money for purchases. They barter in some cases, which means they trade things for other things equal in value.

◆ You can set up a barter trade in your troop or with a group of friends. Bring in several items that you are willing to trade, a book you've already read or a record you're tired of listening to, for example. Each girl sets up her goods in her own section of a room.

After looking at what others have, you can decide on what to trade. For example, Cynthia agrees to trade her truck for Tina's can of tennis balls. You exchange your record for Barbara's comic book.

WEATHER

Weather is the way the air is at a certain time in a particular place. The weather can change from day to day and from month to month. It may be cold one day, hot another; dry and sunny one day, wet and rainy the next. Knowing the weather report for the day gives you the chance to make plans and dress properly. Listen to the weather report on the radio at the start of your day.

Sun

Hooray for the sun! The sun gives heat and light. It dries things and gives Brownie Girl Scouts great days to play. Of course, too much of a good thing can turn out to be not too good. What would happen if it was always sunny? Luckily, Mother Nature also sends rain and snow, too.

▲ Use your hand as a thermometer to see how the sun can heat things. (A thermometer is an instrument that measures how hot or cold something is.) On a hot, sunny day, go outside and feel different objects in the sun and in the shade. Is there a difference? Touch softly first to make sure you don't burn your hand!

◆ Do the same thing with an outdoor thermometer, not the kind used to take a person's temperature. Measure the temperature in the sun and shade to see what the differences are.

◆ Make a list of clothing for hot, sunny weather.

Wind

Wind is moving air. The wind blows all around the earth, bringing all sorts of weather with it. The wind moves and it can move things.

▲ Look outside on a windy day. What is the wind moving? Look at the trees, flags, leaves, loose papers. What is happening to them?

◆ To further see that wind is moving air and that it can move things, make a pinwheel. See pages 162–163 for directions.

You can tell how fast the wind is moving by using this chart. (The section "Storms, Hurricanes, and Tornadoes" on page 119 discusses very dangerous and destructive weather.)

THINGS TO LOOK FOR	WIND SPEED
lakes, ponds, puddles very still; no waves at the ocean; smoke goes straight up; leaves don't move.	0–1 mph calm
ripples on water; small waves; leaves rustle; smoke rises sideways; small flags move; breeze can be felt on face; tall grasses move.	2–10 mph slight breeze
leaves moving; small branches move; papers blow about; small flags wave; small waves on ponds and lakes; tall grasses sway back and forth; good kite-flying weather.	10–20 mph moderate breeze
small trees sway; flags wave; rain or snow falls sideways; wind can be heard; water has waves; papers blow about; dust blows about.	20–30 mph strong breeze
difficult to walk; large trees swaying; twigs break off trees; large waves on water; rain and snow blow sideways. Go indoors to be safe.	30–45 mph gale

117

Clouds and Rain

When there is a lot of water in the air, clouds sometimes form. Clouds are usually moved around by the wind. When the very tiny drops of water get larger and heavier, sometimes they fall to the ground and it rains. Rain is important for plants and animals. Rain fills our lakes, streams, rivers, and reservoirs. Rain can cleanse. Have you ever seen a bird take a bath in the rain?

▲ Go outside on a mildly cloudy day and look at the clouds. Can you see their different shapes? Watch them as they move and change. Look for their different layers. Some clouds are low and some are high. Are they all the same color or do you see several colors?

◆ Make cloud pictures with cotton glued to paper. Imagine the shapes are animals or other things you see when you look at clouds.

▲ Dress properly and go outside and see the changes rain creates. Look at plants, insects, worms, soil, roads, and other things. Where does the rain go? What does it do when if falls?

◆ Make a rain gauge to find out how much rain falls in a storm. Get a jar or glass with straight sides and place it outdoors in a clear area. After the rain has stopped, hold a ruler next to the side of the glass and measure the height of the water. Try the same thing after several rainfalls.

◆ Find out how pollution has caused changes in rain. Learn about acid rain.

Cold Weather

Many parts of the United States get colder in winter because they get less direct sunlight in this season. Sometimes it gets very cold. When the temperature drops low enough, water freezes and becomes ice. When the temperature rises, the ice melts and becomes water again.

Learn how to dress for cold weather in order to keep warm and comfortable.

▲ Find pictures in a magazine, or draw your own pictures, that show what you need to dress for cold weather.

◆ Make a list of necessary cold-weather clothing items.

◆ Make a list of your favorite things to do in cold weather.

Snow

Snowflakes are ice crystals with different shapes and designs that form in clouds in cold weather. When the weather reaches a certain level of coldness and dampness, the ice crystals form flakes that get heavier and larger and finally fall.

▲ Catch some snowflakes on a piece of dark paper or cloth that has been cooled to the outside temperature. Look at the flakes as they lie on the black paper, and see the different crystal designs. If you can, look at them with a magnifying glass.

▲ After a snowstorm, go for a walk and look for animal tracks in the fresh snow. If you are in a rural area, you may find tracks of birds, rabbits, squirrels, and racoons, as well as those of cats, dogs, and people.

Storms, Hurricanes, and Tornadoes

Sometimes the winds and rain become powerful storms, hurricanes, or tornadoes. It is best to be in a safe indoor place when these storms strike. Lightning is a flash of electricity in the sky. It is very powerful and can do a lot of damage. Thunder is the sound you hear when lightning heats up the air so much that the air swells and almost bursts!

During a thunderstorm, it can be exciting to sit inside with your family and listen to the thunder and watch the

119

lightning, but keep away from the windows. Remember these safety rules about lightning:

- Don't stand in an open field. Try to get low to the ground if you can't get inside a building.
- If a lightning storm starts when you are in water, get out and away fast. Seek shelter or lie flat.
- Trees are targets for lightning. Don't stand under them.
- Cars are a safe place to stay.
- Try not to use the telephone and TV during a lightning storm.
- If you are home, close all windows.

A hurricane is a storm with very strong winds and, usually, very heavy rain. A tornado is a very destructive, whirlwind-type storm that looks like a moving funnel twisting out of dark clouds. Weather experts are able to see a bad storm coming by using weather satellites and are usually able to give people advance warning. After such a storm, be careful. Fallen power lines can be very dangerous. Stay out of puddles. The water may be electrified.

 ▲ Think about what animals outside do in bad weather. How do they act? Why?

Weather Calendar

▲ Use a large calendar with the days of the week and the month. Make a record of the weather at the end of each day. If it has been a sunny day, draw a sun on the calendar box for that day. If it has been cloudy, draw a cloud. If it has been rainy, draw rain drops. And if it has been snowy, draw snow. At the end of the month, see how many days of each type of weather you had.

Weather-Watch Hunt

▲ Go for a walk outside and look for the things described in the list below. When you find something on the list, check it off.

See if you can find the following:

- something being warmed by the sun

- a place that is hot
- something in the shade
- a place that is cool
- something blowing in the wind
- something left by the rain
- something wet by the rain
- something that will protect you from rain
- a cloud shaped like an animal
- something with icicles on it
- a snowdrift
- something hidden by snow
- a good place to go in case of a hurricane
- a good place to go in case of a tornado
- a place to protect you from the wind
- an animal that seems to be enjoying the weather.

 ◆ Make up your own list of weather-watch items. Give the list to someone else to try.

Weather Facts from Around the World

- The coldest temperature recorded was near the South Pole, in Vostok. The temperature was 126°F below zero.
- Lightning can strike the same place twice!
- In one flash of lightning, there is enough electricity to light a house for a year.
- Florida gets the most lightning of all the states in the United States of America.
- There is an island in Hawaii where it rains 350 days a year! That island has about 15 days of dry weather each year.
- In the summer, if you count the number of cricket chirps you hear in 15 seconds and add 40 to that number, you will know roughly the temperature at that time.
- The world's highest recorded temperature was in Libya, a country in North Africa. It was around 136°F above zero in the shade!
- No rain has fallen in the Atacama Desert in Chile for over 400 years! It is the driest place in the world.

OUTDOOR SKILLS

The out-of-doors is a special place for you to learn and try new things. Your outdoor adventure may be a nature walk, or you may plan a picnic, or you may go camping. Before you do anything in the out-of-doors, make sure you are ready. Always use this checklist to help you get ready.

1 PLAN AHEAD. Think about what to do. Talk about your plans with your friends and the adults who will go with you.

2 LEARN SKILLS. Learn and practice helpful things—knot tying and pitching tents, for example—before you go.

3 DRESS RIGHT. Make sure your clothes are right for the weather and for what you will be doing.

4 KEEP SAFE. Learn safety rules.

5 WALK SOFTLY. Learn about your environment. Try to leave things just the way they were, or help to make them better.

The outdoor adventures that you'll read about are in steps. Try the steps in order so you can be sure you will be prepared for each new outing.

Outdoor Adventures

1. LOOK OUT Find out about the out-of-doors by talking to people who know about nature and by reading illustrated books about nature.

▲ Learn safety rules. (See pages 91–104.)

▲ Learn what to wear. (See pages 60–61.)

◆ Make a list of things you would like to do in the out-of-doors.

2. MEET OUT Do some easy outdoor things.

▲ Do some of the Try-Its activities in "The World of the Out-of-Doors."

▲ Talk about cooking, hiking, and other outdoor activities.

▲ Go on a plant hike. Try to find as many different plants as you can.

▲ Have a cloud watch. Look for clouds of different shapes and colors.

▲ Look for different shapes in natural things—circles, squares, triangles, ovals, diamonds, straight lines.

▲ Play an outdoor game. (See pages 89–90.)

▲ Explore with a magnifying glass. Look for very small things.

▲ Take a penny hike. Flip a coin. Go right if it is heads and left if it is tails. Do a coin flip every 10 steps.

3. MOVE OUT Find out more about the out-of-doors by doing outdoor things. Your senses can help you learn about the out-of-doors. Sight, smell, touch, and hearing are important in the out-of-doors. Use your senses in these activities.

▲ Touch and guess. Make discoveries with your sense of touch. Do this activity with friends. You'll need a blindfold and rocks, leaves, rice, seeds, feathers, fruits, or other things.

1 Take turns being blindfolded.
2 Give one of the things to the blindfolded girl.
3 Have her try to guess what she is holding.
4 Wet some of the things to make guessing harder.

▲ I hear it. Go on a listening hike in the woods or by the water. Listen carefully. You may hear many different sounds. Do this activity with friends. Can you identify the sources of the sounds you are hearing?

▲ Nosing around. You can learn many things through your sense of smell. Your nose can be a warning system for your body because things that smell bad may also be harmful. Smell as many different outdoor things as you can. Remember not to pick or cut any growing thing. Look for things already on the ground.

124

Here are some ideas:

torn leaf	flowers
wet soil	insects
crushed blade of grass	recently snapped twigs
pond water	wet pieces of wood
pine cones	seashells
pine needles	sand

◆ Seed hunt. Plants start as seeds. Seeds differ in shape and size and can travel, too! For example, dandelion seeds float as if they had parachutes. Maple seeds whirl like helicopter blades. Burs ride piggyback on animals. Violet seeds pop like missiles. Berries are sometimes carried "air mail" by flying birds. Try to find as many different kinds of seeds as you can. Read about them in seed catalogs and take out books on plants from your library.

Remember that good manners are important everywhere, including the out-of-doors. In the woods, for example, you must remember that you are near many other living things and that the out-of-doors is their home. It is important to protect and take care of the environment.

▲ Habitat hunt. Every plant and animal has a home or a place where it lives, called a "habitat." It may be the swamp for an alligator, the forest for a bear, or the beach for a hermit crab. Make a collage, scrapbook, or list of different living things and their homes. Go outside and find a plant or animal. What things are part of its habitat?

125

Help others discover the out-of-doors. Practice describing the things you see and hear outdoors. Doing so will help you look carefully and become better at sharing with others.

▲ Back-to-back. Stand back-to-back with a friend. Pick up something and start describing it to your friend, who has to guess what you are holding. Take turns. This activity can be done indoors, too!

4. EXPLORE OUT   Plan a special outdoor activity. Learn these basic campcraft skills and trail signs skills to help you explore the out-of-doors.

▲ Learn how to make and use these trail signs.

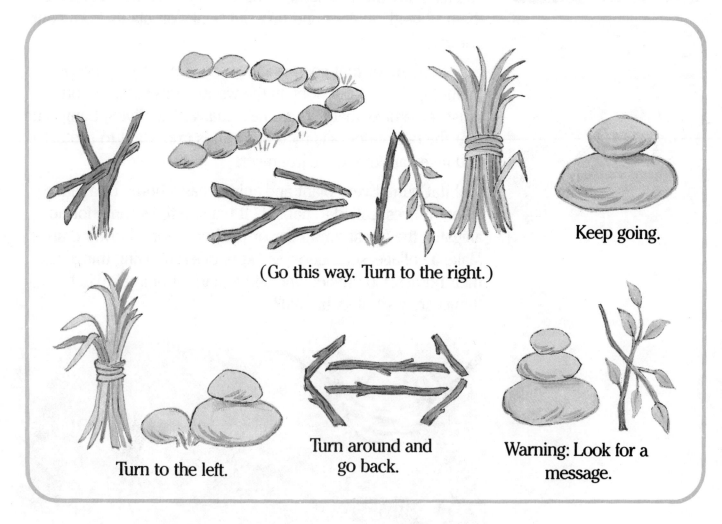

(Go this way. Turn to the right.)

Keep going.

Turn to the left.

Turn around and go back.

Warning: Look for a message.

 ▲ Lay a trail for another group. Hide a nice surprise at the end.

126

Knots

Practice knot tying. You will be able to do many things with these simple knots.

▲ An **overhand knot** is a knot in the end of a rope. This easy knot is made with one piece of rope. Follow the steps in the picture.

◆ A **square knot** is used to tie two ropes together or to tie a package.

1 Tie two pieces of rope together, following the steps in the picture.

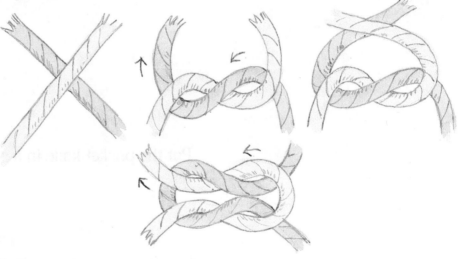

2 Remember this poem:

"Right over left and left over right
Makes the knot neat and tidy and tight."

Using a Pocket Knife

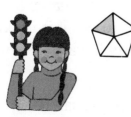

◆ When using a pocket knife, be very careful. Always carry the knife closed.

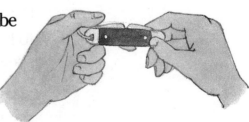

Always close the knife before giving it to someone else and follow these safety tips:

- Use both hands to open the knife.
- Keep fingers behind the cutting blade edge when opening a closing.

- Hold the knife like this.

- Always cut away from your body.

- Put the pocket knife in a safe place when you are not using it.

5. COOK OUT   If you go outdoors for more than a few hours, you will probably want something to eat. It is important to know how to make snacks that are easy to carry and won't spoil.

▲ Have a picnic. Take along foods you have prepared. See pages 57–60.

Snacks to Take Along

A fruit-and-nut mix is a good snack to take along. The ingredients are raisins, peanuts, dried cereal, dried fruit, walnuts, almonds, and coconut flakes. Mix together any or all of these ingredients. Provide everyone with her own snack bag.

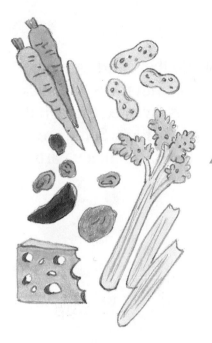

▲ Walking salad—carrots, celery, or cucumbers; cheese slices; green beans; zucchini; squash; cauliflower; broccoli; peanut butter. Clean and cut the vegetables into sticks or small chunks. You can even spread peanut butter inside the celery sticks. Put the salad sticks in plastic bags.

Once you are ready to spend a whole day on an outdoor adventure, you will need to know how to do some outdoor cooking. Never cook without an adult to help you.

◆ Plan a cookout. Pack foods you will cook outdoors.

6. SLEEP OUT After you have practiced many things in the out-of-doors, you can start to think about an overnight camping trip. But before you go, you'll have to make plans and practice some skills.

▲ Have a slumber party.
▲ Find out about sleeping bags or bedrolls. Learn how to roll and tie one.
▲ Try sleeping at home in a sleeping bag or bedroll.
◆ Sleep out in a backyard.

129

TOOLS

A tool is something that helps people do their work. A long time ago, people made very simple tools with rocks and sticks. Tools have been improved and new ones invented through the ages. To this day, we are still inventing new tools. Some are very simple, and others are giant machines with many parts.

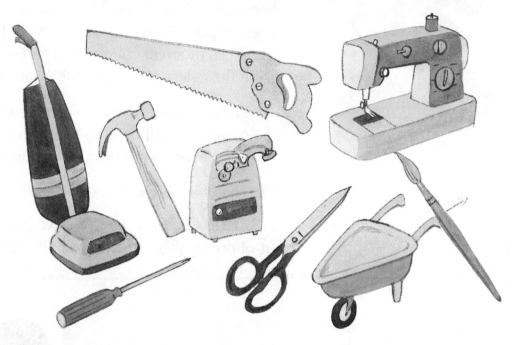

▲ Guess which tools are being described below. The answers are in the box at the end.

1 I am used to pound nails into wood. I can also remove nails from wood.
2 I have teeth that can cut wood into pieces.
3 I have a handle and am used to put screws into wood. I also remove screws.
4 I am straight as an arrow with stripes on my sides. My stripes are very neat, and I help you keep things that way. I come in different sizes. Sometimes I have only one foot.
5 I have hairs called bristles. They can spread paint on walls, wood, paper, and other surfaces.
6 I can be used to cut things. I can fold in half and I am very useful to have on a camping trip.

Answers: 1. hammer 2. saw 3. screwdriver 4. ruler 5. paintbrush 6. jackknife

130

▲ Have a tool hunt in and around your home. Try to learn how some of the tools are used.

Using Tools to Make Things

You can make many things with tools, but first learn how to use them.

Follow these safety tips:

1 Have an adult show you how to use tools.
2 Make sure you have space to work.
3 Use the right tools for the job. Using a tool for something it wasn't meant to do can be dangerous.
4 Tools are not toys. They can be fun to use but are not for play.
5 Don't use broken tools. They can be dangerous.

▲ Practice hammering nails and sawing old pieces of scrap wood. Then go on to the next activity.

◆ Board tic-tac-toe is a board game that you can make for your room. You will need 1 square flat board, 9 1-inch nails, 5 large, identical buttons, 5 identical buttons of a different color than the other five, a ruler, pencil, ink marker, sheet of sandpaper, hammer, and 10 twist ties for closing plastic bags.

Do the following:

1 Have someone help you make the board 12 inches wide and 12 inches long.
2 Draw lines like those in the drawing.

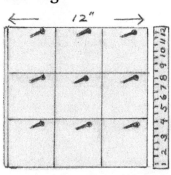

3 Hammer a nail in the top part of each box.
4 Poke a twist tie through each button.

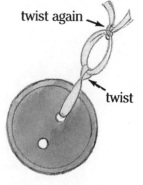

twist again

twist

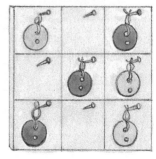

5 You are now ready to play.
6 Each person gets five buttons of the same color. Take turns hanging buttons on the nails instead of writing Xs and Os. The first one to get three of her color in a row wins. Take the buttons down and start again.

ON MY OWN

The adults in your family may not always be around to take care of you. You may walk alone to and from school. You may play outside or go to the playground alone. You may spend time at home alone. At these times you must look after yourself and protect yourself from harm. It's a big job, but looking after yourself can be lots of fun. To do a good job of taking care of yourself when an adult is not with you, you must know the same things that a baby-sitter must know. Why? Because you become your own baby-sitter! You must know the following:

- the family rules (what the adults in your family expect of you when they are not around).
- what to do in case of an emergency. Be sure to read pages 98–99.
- first aid. Be sure to read pages 107–110.

Knowing these things will help you feel safe and keep you and your family from worrying. This knowledge will also make it easier for you to have safe fun when you are alone.

132

Games for You

How do you use the time you spend at home alone? Maybe you have chores or homework to do. You may have a favorite game or toy. Try some of the fun games and activities that follow. You can do these alone.

 ▲ Dance the time away! Dancing is great exercise. It can help keep you in shape. Practice some of the new dance steps. If you have permission to play records or the radio, put on some music and dance, dance, dance!

 ▲ Read a book. Reading is a great way to spend your time. Visit the library often. Ask your librarian or a parent to suggest a good book to check out. Always have one ready for your time alone.

 ▲ Make a montage. A montage is a number of pictures pasted together on a piece of cardboard or a sturdy surface. Tell a story about yourself, a friend, your family, or the area where you live. Or make a picture of a house, an animal, or anything you like. You will need a piece of heavy paper or cardboard, some paste or glue, and lots of imagination.

Look through old newspapers and magazines for pictures to cut out. Look around the house for things you can use, too.

Imagine making a building or animal with the following: paper clips, ticket stubs, small plastic toys that you don't play with anymore, empty thread spools, old keys, buttons, shells, pebbles, dried leaves, paper plates, paper cups, scraps of wrapping paper, bottle tops, rubber bands, cotton balls. Find a box to store these things and get permission to use them. And plan ahead, so that when you decide to start this project, everything is ready!

◆ Pick a word, any word. Open any book and pick out a long word (10 letters or more). Write that word at the top of a blank sheet of paper. Look at the letters in this word and try to make other words. For example, with the letters in the word "refrigerator," you can make the words "get," "to," and "eat." Do you see any others?

▲ Pick up clips. Grab a handful of paper clips (15 clips or more). Pull out the smaller loop in each clip to form a funny-looking "V." Here is how you play:

1 Hold all the clips in your hand and shake them.
2 Drop the clips on a table or the floor.
3 Try to pick up the clips by hooking them on one clip.

BRIDGING

Moving from one age level to another is called **bridging**. You will "cross the bridge" from Brownie to Junior Girl Scouting, the next age level, at the end of your last year as a Brownie Girl Scout. You might have bridged from Daisy Girl Scouting when you became a Brownie Girl Scout and so already know something about bridging.

You can prepare for Junior Girl Scouting by working on the bridging steps in this chapter, which will earn you the Bridge to Junior Girl Scouts patch.

HELPING DAISY GIRL SCOUTS

Throughout your Brownie Girl Scout years, you will be able to help Daisy Girl Scouts with their bridging. You can visit their troop meetings and tell them about Brownie Girl Scouting.

Other things you can do to help Daisy Girl Scouts are the following:

▲ Help at Daisy Girl Scout meetings. Wear your Brownie Girl Scout uniform to their meetings and tell Daisy Girl Scouts about the Try-Its patches and membership pins.

◆ Become a pen pal to a Daisy Girl Scout, and keep her up-to-date about what you are doing in Girl Scouting.

▲ Tell or act out the Brownie Girl Scout story to a Daisy Girl Scout.

▲ Help Daisy Girl Scouts make friends with other Brownie Girl Scouts.

▲ Go on a trip with Daisy Girl Scouts.

▲ Invite Daisy Girl Scouts to your Brownie Girl Scout meetings.

▲ Help Daisy Girl Scouts plan their bridging ceremony to Brownie Girl Scouting.

BECOMING A JUNIOR GIRL SCOUT

As a Brownie Girl Scout, you have had fun, made friends, and learned new things. Now it's time to look forward to Junior Girl Scouting! To help you become a Junior Girl Scout, you may take part in bridging activities during your last year as a Brownie Girl Scout.

BRIDGE TO JUNIOR GIRL SCOUTS PATCH

To earn the Bridge to Junior Girl Scouts patch, you must do at least one activity from each of the seven bridging steps. Do these bridging steps in the order that they are numbered. You may make up your own activities for each bridging step.

Bridge to Junior Girl Scouts patch

Seven Bridging Steps

Bridging step one—Find out about Junior Girl Scouting.

- Invite an adult who works with Junior Girl Scouts to tell you about Junior Girl Scouting. Find out how you can become a Junior Girl Scout.
- Invite a Junior Girl Scout to also tell you about Junior Girl Scouting.
- Find a Junior Girl Scout to be your "big sister" and help you with bridging activities.
- Look through the *Junior Girl Scout Handbook* and *Girl Scout Badges and Signs*. Read about the membership pin that Junior Girl Scouts wear and the recognitions that they may earn.
- Look at the uniform and recognitions for Junior Girl Scouts.

Bridging step two—Do a Junior Girl Scout activity.

- Do a Junior Girl Scout badge activity from *Girl Scout Badges and Signs*.
- Do an activity from the *Junior Girl Scout Handbook*. (You may do a badge activity from the handbook.)
- Make something described in the *Junior Girl Scout Handbook*.
- Do a service activity that a Junior Girl Scout might do.

Bridging step three—Do something with a Junior Girl Scout.

- Go on a field trip.
- Do a service project.
- Make something, using your camping skills.
- Make some food to share with other girls.
- Find and write to a Junior Girl Scout pen pal.
- Learn a new song or game that Junior Girl Scouts sing or play.
- Make something described in the *Junior Girl Scout Handbook*.

Bridging step four—Share what you learn about Junior Girl Scouting with Brownie or Daisy Girl Scouts.

- Make a collage about Junior Girl Scouting for your Brownie or Daisy Girl Scout friends.
- Show them a Junior Girl Scout activity.
- Tell them about a field trip or service project that you did with a Junior Girl Scout.
- Teach them a song or game that you learned from a Junior Girl Scout.

Bridging step five—Do Junior Girl Scout recognition activities.

- Earn a Dabbler badge from one of the worlds of interest in *Girl Scout Badges and Signs.*
- Do one of the following badges from *Girl Scout Badges and Signs*: Individual Sports, My Heritage, Science Sleuth, Dance, or Outdoor Fun.
- Do a badge activity from each world of interest in *Girl Scout Badges and Signs.*
- Do one activity from five different badges in the *Junior Girl Scout Handbook.*

Bridging step six—Help plan your bridging (fly-up) ceremony. See pages 34–36 for some ideas.

- Learn how to do an opening or closing for a ceremony that is different from any opening or closing you have done before.

- Write a poem about Brownie or Junior Girl Scouting.
- Make up a song for the ceremony.
- Design and make invitations for the ceremony.
- Make decorations to be used at the ceremony.

Bridging step seven—Plan and do a summer Girl Scout activity. If your Girl Scout group has its Court of Awards before summer, you may be able to get your Bridge to Junior Girl Scouts patch then. Remember to promise to do step seven over the summer.

- Go to Girl Scout camp.
- Plan and go on a picnic with some other Girl Scouts.
- Have a camp fire or cookout with other Girl Scouts.
- Make a summer scrapbook to share with your new Junior Girl Scout friends.
- Have a sports day with other Girl Scouts.
- Plan a get-acquainted activity that you can do in the fall with your new Junior Girl Scout friends.
- Write a summer newsletter.
- Send postcards to your Brownie Girl Scout friends.
- Be ready to let your Junior Girl Scout friends know about your summer.

LOOKING BACK AND LOOKING AHEAD

Brownie Girl Scouts who become Junior Girl Scouts receive Brownie Girl Scout wings, which are sewn onto the Junior Girl Scout uniform. Girls who join Junior Girl Scouting without first being Brownie Girl Scouts do not receive Brownie Girl Scout wings. They may ask you about your wings. Here's the story behind Brownie Girl Scout wings:

Brownie Girl Scout Wings

A long time ago, Brownie Girl Scout leaders were called "Brown Owls." At the fly-up ceremony, the Brown Owl gave those girls in her troop who were ready to go to the next age level in Girl Scouting their wings to "fly up." The same ceremony is still done today, even though Brownie Girl Scout leaders aren't called Brown Owls anymore.

At a fly-up ceremony, you receive your wings and renew your Girl Scout Promise and get the membership pin that is worn by Junior, Cadette, Senior, and adult Girl Scouts. You will have a chance to plan your fly-up ceremony with the girls in your troop and with the Junior Girl Scouts in the troop you will be joining.

Girl Scout membership pin

Each step of Junior Girl Scouting can be filled with fun and adventure. There are 94 badges and 4 signs you can work on as a Junior Girl Scout, or you can invent your own badge and develop an "Our Own Troop's" badge. You can also earn the Junior Aide patch by helping Brownie Girl Scouts bridge to Junior Girl Scouting. The *Junior Girl Scout Handbook* has a lot of information and fun activities for you and your Junior Girl Scout friends. The possibilities are many!

Sign of the World

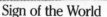

Junior Aide patch

KEEPING TRACK OF YOUR BROWNIE GIRL SCOUT FRIENDS

Your copy of the *Brownie Girl Scout Handbook* has been a record of your times in Brownie Girl Scouting. You may have made many good friends with whom you want to keep in touch. Some friends may be going with you into Junior Girl

Scouting; some may be moving; some may be continuing in Brownie Girl Scouting. Use this space for their autographs, poems, thoughts, drawings—whatever they want to write for you in your copy of the *Brownie Girl Scout Handbook*. You'll be able to look at it later on and remember your Brownie Girl Scout days.

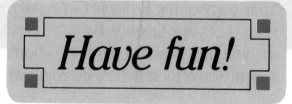

Have fun!

BROWNIE GIRL SCOUT TRY-ITS

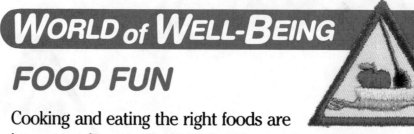

Getting started on new adventures can be fun. This section has many new ideas and activities, called Try-Its. There are 15 different Try-Its—three for each of the five worlds of interest. For each type of Try-It, you have six activities to choose from. When you have done four activities in one Try-It, you will get a patch for that Try-It to wear on your Brownie Girl Scout sash.

You may be able to do many of the Try-Its on your own. Sometimes you will need help from others. Try to do them with your friends.

WORLD of WELL-BEING

FOOD FUN

Cooking and eating the right foods are important for your health. Cooking and preparing food are fun, too!

FRUIT PIE   Make an apple pie. You will need the following:

6 big, tart apples (baking apples)
½ cup sugar
1 teaspoon of cinnamon
1½ tablespoons of flour
2 defrosted, ready-made pie shells
mixing bowl, large spoons, fork, knife, peeler.

1 Preheat the oven to 375°F.
2 Peel the apples. Take out the core. Cut the apples into small pieces and put them into the mixing bowl.
3 Add the cinnamon, flour, and sugar to the apples and mix.
4 Fill one of the ready-made pie shells with the apple mixture.
5 Take the other pie shell out of its tin. Put the shell on top of the apple mixture. Close the pie up by pressing your fork along the edge. Poke a few holes in the top of the pie with your fork so that hot air can get out as it bakes.
6 Bake the pie in the oven for one hour. The crust should be light brown and the apples should be cooked by then.
7 After the pie has been baked and has cooled off a bit, it is ready to eat.
8 Be sure to clean up afterwards.

FOOD CHART It's fun to keep track of what you eat. Try making a food chart for a day. You will need your handbook, a pencil or markers, and paper for the chart.

1 Read pages 57–60 from the chapter "Taking Care of Myself."
2 Make a chart like the one on page 58. Keep track of what you're eating for one day.

BROWNIE GIRL SCOUT STEW Make this great and easy recipe for indoor or outdoor cooking! It will serve three or more girls. You will need three same-size cans of food: one can of soup, one can of vegetables, and one can of meat or a can of beans like chick peas or kidney beans. You will also need a can opener, a large spoon for stirring, a large pot, bowls, and spoons.

1 Open all cans with a can opener.
2 Pour the soup, vegetable, and meat or beans into the pot and stir.
3 Add one cup of water.
4 Heat until hot.
5 Serve.
6 Clean up.

SNACKS FOR GIRL SCOUTS Try these two snacks at Girl Scout get-togethers.
1. Vegetable Snacks. Make the walking salad on page 129 in "Outdoor Skills."

2. Fruit Juice Fizz. You will need one orange or lemon, orange juice, pineapple juice, cranberry juice, seltzer or club soda, a bowl or pitcher, and a knife.

1 Cut the orange (or lemon) into slices.
2 Put one or two cups of each juice into the pitcher.
3 Add three more cups of juice for every cup of seltzer or club soda.
4 Chill the juice.
5 Serve.

FOOD FOR A DAY   Make your own breakfast, lunch, and dinner for a day. Use recipes that are your favorites. Ask an adult for help.

WORLD FOODS   Try some fun recipes enjoyed by people around the world. Find and make a favorite recipe from another country.

WORLD of WELL-BEING

DANCERCIZE

Physical exercise helps keep our bodies healthy. Some exercises can be done to music. You can help keep yourself fit by doing the following dance and movement exercises.

ANIMAL MOVES   You will need your *Brownie Girl Scout Handbook* and music for this animal movement exercise.

1 Read pages 53–55 in the chapter "Taking Care of Myself."

2 To the beat of the music, move your body like a rabbit, crab, elephant, seal, inchworm, frog, and other animals.

LUMMI STICKS   Learn how to play and dance to the beat of lummi sticks. Do the lummi stick activity on page 94 of the chapter "My World."

MY OWN DANCE   Make up a dance to your favorite rhyme or song. You'll need a book of rhymes or songs.

1 Pick a favorite rhyme or song.
2 Make up your own dance steps to go with the words.
3 Pick music to go with the rhyme, or sing and dance to your song.

SAN SERENI Learn the San Sereni singing game in the chapter "My World."

AEROBIC DANCE Try dancing as a way to keep fit and have fun. "Aerobic" (Air-row-bic) activity makes you breathe hard and fast and helps make your heart stronger. You'll need a record or tape, record player or tape player, shorts and T-shirt or leotards and tights, and gym sneakers.

1 Do the exercises on pages 53–55 to get your body ready for dancing.
2 Practice these movements without music:
   - Jog in place.
   - Step forward or backward and swing your arms to the sides.

- Step sideways and swing your arms in circles.
- Put your hands on your hips and move from side to side.
- Walk in a circle, lifting your knees very high while clapping your hands.

3 Now do the steps to music. Repeat several times. Dance for 5 to 10 minutes.

DANCE PARTY   Have a dancing party with a group of friends. You'll need records or tapes, a record player or tape player, and snacks.

1 Pick a time and a place for a get-together with your friends.

2 Decide on the music. Each person can bring her favorite dance music.

3 Teach each other dance steps.

WORLD of WELL-BEING

SPORTS AND GAMES

BALL GAMES   Many sports are played with balls. Try these exercises with at least two kinds of round balls, such as a baseball and a basketball. You'll also need your *Brownie Girl Scout Handbook*. Practice each of these steps.

1 Toss the ball back and forth from your right hand to your left hand.

2 Bounce the ball with your right hand, then with your left hand.

3 Throw the ball in the air and catch it with two hands.

4 Throw the ball up and catch it after one bounce on the ground.

5 Throw the ball against a wall and then catch it.

6 Throw the ball into a box or basket.

7 Throw the ball as far as you can.

8 Throw the ball as high as you can.

9 Play catch with someone.

SWIMMING Have an adult teach you how to swim.

Always remember the following:
- Have an adult watching you.
- Swim with a buddy.
- Swim where there are a lifeguard and rescue equipment.
- Leave the water before you get tired or cold.
- Wear a personal-flotation device.

You'll need a swimsuit, water (pool, beach, or lake), and an adult to watch. Ask her or him to help you practice these swimming skills.

1 Sit down in knee-deep water with feet and legs in front of you and hands behind you on the bottom. Move your head back slightly. Straighten your legs and raise your feet.

2 Kneel in water up to your knees. Hold your friend's hand for balance. Put your head into the water and see if you can hold your breath to the count of 10. Try this when holding your nose and without holding it. See if you can keep your eyes open when underwater.

3 See how long you can tread water. Move your arms and legs underwater. Keep your head above the water and your body straight.

BICYCLING   Bicycling is fun and good exercise. If you have a bicycle, try these bicycling skills.

1 Ride your bicycle as slowly as you can without stopping.
2 Ride your bicycle in circles. Try to make the circles as small as you can.
3 Ride your bicycle in a long, straight line.
4 Practice turning, using hand signals. Put your right hand straight out to your right side to turn right, your left hand straight out to your left side to turn left.
5 Set up a bicycling practice course. Place 10–20 large metal cans in a wide play area. Try to ride around the course without touching the cans. The picture will give you ideas on how to set up your course.

SKATING   Ice skating and roller skating are fun sports and are good for fitness. Always skate with a buddy and follow safety rules. You'll need a pair of skates and comfortable clothes.

1 Practice falling. Stand in your skates and bend your knees so you are squatting. Bend backward a little and fall on your bottom. Extend your arms in front of you.

2 Skate forward, to your left, to your right, around corners, and stop.

3 Skate backward, to your left, to your right, around corners, and stop.

4 Skate forward and backward to music with a partner.

PAPER KICK BALL   Your feet are very important for many sports and games. Try this football game with your friends. You'll need one large brown paper bag and four or more players.

1 Press the brown paper bag into a ball.

2 All the players stand in a circle.

3 Choose one player to be the first kicker.

4 The first kicker kicks the paper ball to someone she names in the circle.

5 The ball keeps getting kicked until someone misses it and it goes outside the circle.

6 The person who misses the ball gets a point. She then kicks the ball to someone else.

7 The winner is the player with the lowest number of points.

GAMES   Read pages 56–57 in the section "Taking Care of Myself" and play two of the games.

PEOPLE OF THE WORLD

You share the earth with many people. People can take better care of this world if they know and understand each other better. Try these activities to learn more about people.

HELLO, GOOD-BYE   Learn how to say hello and good-bye in other languages. You will need someone to help you learn to say these words correctly. A guide for how to say these words in French, Spanish, and Swahili is shown below. Ask someone who speaks Chinese, Polish, and other languages how they say hello and good-bye.

1	Hello	Good-bye
French	bonjour (bohn-joor)	au revoir (oh-rev-wa)
Spanish	hola (oh-lah)	hasta la vista (ahs-tah la vees-tah)
Swahili	jambo (djahm-boh)	kwahire (kwah-he-ree)

2 Teach these new words to your friends and family.

MR. BEAR   Play the Swedish game called Mr. Bear with friends. Read pages 89–90 to find out how.

SONGS   Learn how to sing three of the songs on pages 90–92.

WORLD STORIES   Use some facts and your imagination to take a trip around the world. You will need a map of the world and books about different countries.

1 Close your eyes and put your finger on a spot on the map.
2 Read a book about the place you picked.
3 Tell someone about the things you learned.

UNITED STATES OF AMERICA MONTAGE   Do the United States of America montage on page 88 in the chapter "My World."

CLOTHING AROUND THE WORLD   Read about "My Country and My World" and do the clothing and uniform activities on pages 86–87.

WORLD of PEOPLE

PLAY

People all over the world have ways to relax and play. Here are some games for you to try that children in other countries play.

KIM'S GAME (ENGLAND)   Girl Scouts and Girl Guides all over the world play this game. You'll need one or more friends to play with, at least 10 small things, and a scarf.

1 Put 10 things on a table. Be sure you can cover all of them with the scarf.
2 Show the players the 10 things for one minute. Then cover them with the scarf.
3 Ask the players what was on the table. See if they can list all 10 things.

JAN-KEN-PON (JAPAN)   This is a fun game played in Japan. Look on page 89 of "My World" for directions on how to play it.

SHEEP AND HYENA (SUDAN)   See if you can keep the sheep away from the hungry hyena! You'll need at least 10 people—the more the better.

1 Players join hands and form a tight circle.
2 One player stays outside the circle. She is the hyena.
3 Another player stays inside the circle. She is the sheep.

4 The players in the circle have to try to keep the hyena from breaking through the circle to get to the sheep. The game ends when the hyena gets the sheep or gets too tired to go after the sheep anymore.

5 Two other people become the sheep and the hyena.

MR. BEAR (SWEDEN) The moral of this game is "Watch out for sleeping bears!" Look on pages 89–90 to find out how to play this fun game.

RED LIGHT, GREEN LIGHT (UNITED STATES OF AMERICA) Here is one of many ways to play this game.

1 Choose someone to be It. The person who is It stands far away from all the other players at one end of the playing field.

2 The others line up along the starting line at the other end of the field.

3 It turns her back to the group and yells "green light." The players may now run toward It.

4 When It yells "red light," everyone must stop running and freeze. It turns around right after she yells "red light." If It catches anyone moving, that person has to go back to the starting line.

5 The game continues until someone has been able to reach and touch It while It has her back turned to the group.

6 That person becomes It.

HAWK AND HENS (ZIMBABWE) This is a great chasing game for times when you have lots of energy and want to run. See page 90 for directions on how to play.

WORLD of PEOPLE

GIRL SCOUT WAYS

This section contains activities that involve hand signs, sayings, ceremonies, and other things that help make Girl Scouting a special experience.

GIRL SCOUT HAND SIGNS The following are some hand signs that have meaning for Girl Scouts everywhere. Read about these hand signs in the chapter "Girl Scouting." Practice them:

Girl Scout handshake	talking sign
Girl Scout sign	friendship circle
quiet sign	friendship squeeze.

GIRL SCOUT SAYINGS Girl Scout sayings express the ways you hope to act and be as a Girl Scout.

1 Reread the section "The Girl Scout Promise and Law" on pages 5–12.

2 Reread the Girl Scout motto and slogan in the section "Special Girl Scout Ways." See pages 13–14.

3 Demonstrate the Girl Scout Promise and Law, the motto, and the slogan in your daily life.

CEREMONIES   Girl Scout ceremonies are special. You can practice doing some of them in this activity. You will need this handbook.

1 Read about Girl Scout ceremonies on pages 34–36.
2 Plan and carry out a ceremony with your group.

GIRL SCOUT BIRTHDAY   Juliette Low started the first Girl Scout troop on March 12, 1912. This day is the Girl Scout birthday. Plan a party on this day. See page 37 for more ideas.

HIKING STICK   Make a hiking stick and decorate it. You will need a straight stick cut to a comfortable walking-stick length, paint, and brushes.

1 Paint words, symbols, images, or designs on the stick to represent your name or nickname, your hobby, your pet, or some other things.
2 Share the meaning of the artwork on your hiking stick with your friends.
3 Go on a hike with your walking stick.

SIT-UPON   Girl Scouts make sit-upons to use when the ground is damp or to keep their clothes clean. You'll need a large piece of waterproof material (an old vinyl or plastic tablecloth or shower curtain works fine), newspapers or stuffing, a yarn needle, and yarn or string.

1 Cut the waterproof material into two large squares big enough for you to sit on.
2 Place newspapers or old rags between the two squares to form a cushion.
3 Sew the two squares together with yarn or string, using the yarn needle. Be sure to sew completely around the edges of the sit-upon. See the picture.

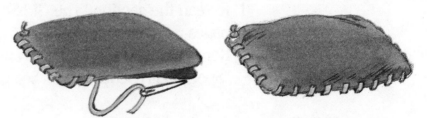

SCIENCE MAGIC

Try these activities to see science in action. The changes seem like magic, but a scientist can make them happen.

HOME-GROWN CRYSTALS   Crystals are minerals that are clear and sparkly. Ice, salt, and diamonds have colors, too! Try growing some of your own mineral crystals. You'll need a container of Epsom salt, two cups of hot water, a bowl, charcoal briquets or pieces of brick, a spoon, and food coloring.

1 Add one-half cup of Epsom salt to the two cups of hot water in the bowl.
2 Stir the Epsom salt and water for about three minutes.
3 Put two or three charcoal briquets or pieces of brick into the bowl.
4 Place your bowl where you can look at it but won't have to move it for five days.
5 Look in on your growing crystals at least once a day.
6 The crystals on the charcoal briquet or pieces of brick are from the Epsom salt.
7 Make your crystals grow in colors by putting one or two drops of food coloring on the charcoal or brick when you begin and before you set the bowl aside.

More to do: Look for crystals outdoors. Many rocks have crystals. A magnifying glass will help you see them.

MAKING BUTTER   You can get different foods from cream. Try this experiment to see how you can change cream into butter. You'll need a small container of heavy cream at room temperature, a large, clean glass jar (a big peanut butter jar is good), ice cubes, a strainer, a small cup, and a spoon.

1 Pour the cream into the clean jar.
2 Add three or four ice cubes.
3 Cover the jar with the top. Be sure the top is turned tightly.

4 Hold your jar and shake it for about 15 minutes, or until you see little bits of butter in the cream. Share the shaking with a friend.

5 Put the jar in the refrigerator for one hour.

6 Empty the jar through a strainer. Is there something you can make with the watery buttermilk that is left over?

7 Pour some very cold, clean water over the butter bits.

8 Carefully spoon the butter bits into the small cup.

9 Spread your butter on some bread or crackers.

10 Eat it.

HOMEMADE RECYCLED PAPER   Make your own paper by doing the activity on pages 84–86 in the chapter "My World."

CHEMISTRY MAGIC   Try this experiment to see how chemicals can change things. You'll need a glass or plastic cup, white vinegar, salt, some old pennies, and iron nails.

1 tsp. salt

← vinegar

1 Put about 5 to 10 pennies in the cup.

2 Put vinegar in the cup. Make sure the pennies are covered by the vinegar.

3 Add one teaspoon of salt.

4 Swirl everything around.

5 Your pennies will become shiny because the vinegar and salt can dissolve tarnish.

6 Take the pennies out of the cup.

7 Put one or two nails into the salty vinegar and wait five minutes.

8 The copper comes from the dissolved tarnish in the salty vinegar. This will coat the nail.

More to do: Try this experiment with nickels or other coins or pieces of metal.

MAGNET HUNT   Magnets can pull things to them. Most magnets are made of iron and come in many different shapes. Not everything will stick to a magnet. Get a magnet and find out what will stick to it.

1 Take your magnet and touch it to as many different things as you can find.

2 Write down all the things that are pulled to the magnet and all those that are not.

MAGNET PULLS   MAGNET DOESN'T PULL

_____   _____

_____   _____

_____   _____

_____   _____

_____   _____

More to do: Find something small that is pulled to a magnet. Try paper clips or straight pins. See how many you can lift with your magnet. Try this experiment with a friend who has her own magnet.

STATIC ELECTRICITY A special kind of electricity, called static electricity, can be made by rubbing some things together. Lightning is a kind of static electricity in the clouds. The spark you sometimes feel when you touch something after walking on a rug is static electricity. To make static electricity, you'll need balloons, string, very small pieces of paper, and wool cloth.

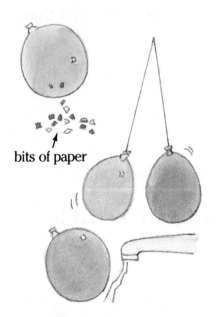

bits of paper

1 Blow up the balloons and tie the ends.
2 Make static electricity by rubbing a balloon very quickly on the wool cloth. You can use your hair instead of the wool cloth.
3 Hold the balloon over the very small pieces of paper to see static electricity in action.
4 Take two more balloons and tie a piece of string to each one.
5 Rub the balloons on the wool cloth.

6 Hold the balloons by the string and try to make them touch.
7 Rub another balloon on the wool cloth.
8 Hold the balloon next to a thin stream of water from a faucet. What happens?
9 Hold this balloon to the wall. If it has enough static electricity, it will stick. Rub the balloon to give it more static charges.

More to do: You can see and hear static electricity. Do this experiment if you have a clothes dryer. Put wet clothes in the dryer and run it. When the clothes are finished drying, make the room as dark as you can. Take the clothes out of the dryer. See what happens. After your experiment, help fold the clothes.

WORLD of TODAY AND TOMORROW

MOVERS

You can move in many ways. You can fly through the air, float on water, or roll along on land, for example. Try making the things listed below to see some of the ways things can move.

WIND WHEELS Try this experiment to see how moving air has energy to move things. You'll need square sheets of stiff paper, straight pins, and straws or thin wooden sticks eight or more inches long.

1 Cut paper squares, following the dotted lines on the diagram.
2 Fold the bottom right-hand corner up to the center, but don't press to make a crease.

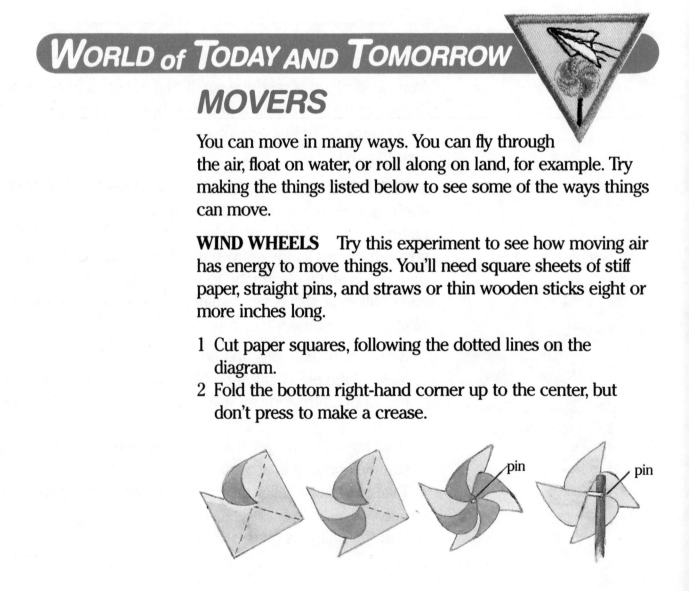

3 Then go around to the other three corners and fold them the same way.

4 Poke the pin through the middle of the paper and then into the end of the straw or stick.

5 If the point comes through the straw or stick, cover the point with clay, glue, or other material, or bend the end down and cover with tape.

You can decorate the paper before making the wind wheel. Find out the different ways you can make the machine spin. Hold it over a lighted light bulb. Blow on it. Run with it. What happens? Your wind wheel is a pinwheel.

Find out about windmills—where they are, what they are used for, and how they work.

FLIERS   Try making these paper fliers. The air holds them up and their shape makes them fly in different patterns. You'll need sheets of paper the size of this book (construction paper or magazine covers work well), scissors, straw, tape, and paper clips.

I. Helicopter

1 Cut the paper in half the long way. You'll only need one of these halves.

2 Fold the paper in half the long way, then fold in half the long way again.

3 Fold the paper in the middle.

4 Fold the ends, as the diagram shows.

5 Weight the bottom with a paper clip.

6 Drop your helicopter from a high point to see it fly.

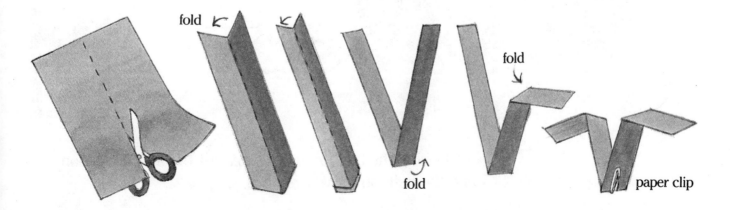

fold   fold   fold   fold   paper clip

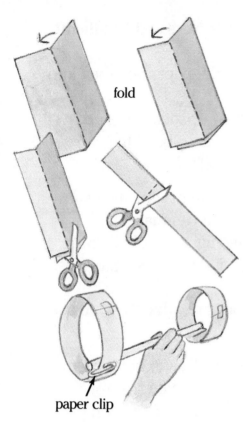

fold

paper clip

II. Circle Glider

1 Fold a piece of paper in half the long way. Fold it in half the long way again.
2 Make two strips by cutting along the folds. Give a friend the other strips for her glider.
3 Cut the width of one of your strips in half.
4 Make a loop with the long strip, and paperclip it to the straw. Put the small hoop of the clip into the straw.
5 Loop the half-strip and paperclip it to the other end of the straw.
6 With the short loop facing forward, give your glider a quick toss to send it flying.

Find out more about paper gliders and paper kites.

BALLOON ROCKET   Try making this balloon rocket to see how air can move things. You'll need a large balloon, tape, a plastic straw, and six feet or more of string.

1 Wet the string and pull it straight. Thread the string through the straw.
2 Tie each end of the string to something—a chair, for example.
3 Stretch the string straight.
4 Blow up the balloon and hold the opening closed.
5 Tape the balloon to the straw.
6 Let go of the balloon.

string

straw   tape

7 Air leaving the balloon pushes against the air in the room, and the balloon moves forward.

Find out about space shuttles and rockets. Check for books from your library.

MOVING SEEDS   Do the activity on page 125 to find out how seeds move and spread.

CLOUDS   See how the wind moves clouds. Read pages 116–118. Do two of the activities on page 117 of the chapter "Things to Know."

TWIG RAFTS   These small rafts are like bigger ones used to cross rivers and streams years ago. You can sail them in the bathtub or pool or on a waterway. You'll need 14 straight twigs or sticks each 10 inches long. You'll also need string, white glue, and stiff paper or cellophane.

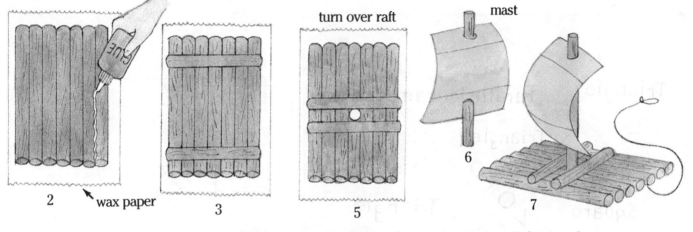

1 Follow the drawings. Line up seven sticks on the wax paper.
2 Squeeze glue between the sticks.
3 Let the glue dry.
4 Lay down two sticks on each end and glue.
5 After the glue dries, turn over the raft and glue down two more sticks.
6 Make a sail by pushing the paper onto the last stick. These will be the mast and sail for sailing.
7 Glue the mast down between one of the cross-sticks and put the last one next to it.
8 Tie the string to one end of the raft so you can keep it from floating away.

More to try: Decorate your sail. To make the raft look more like a real one, bind the raft sticks with string instead of glue.

NUMBERS AND SHAPES

Numbers and shapes are important to people who study mathematics. You can have fun with them, too. Try these activities to see for yourself.

MATH SHAPES   Try to make different patterns from the same shapes. You'll need paper, scissors, a ruler, and a pencil.

1 Have someone help you trace or draw the different shapes inside the square.

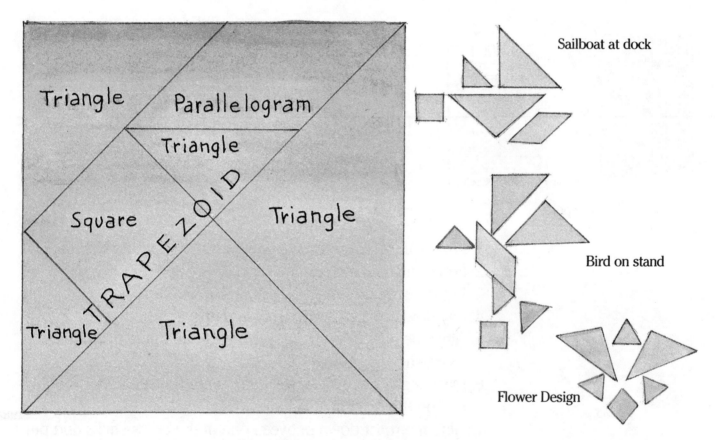

Sailboat at dock

Bird on stand

Flower Design

2 Cut the paper on the lines.
3 Try to put your shapes back into the same square.
4 Try to make other patterns and designs.

You will find out more about shapes, like triangles and rectangles, when you study geometry (gee-om-eh-tree).

MÖBIUS STRIPS   Simple paper magic can happen with "Möbius (mo-bee-us) strips." (These paper twists are named after the German mathematician August F. Möbius.) You'll need sheets of newspaper, scissors, tape, a ruler, and a pencil.

1 Draw long, straight lines on the paper. Use the ruler to help you space the lines and draw them straight.

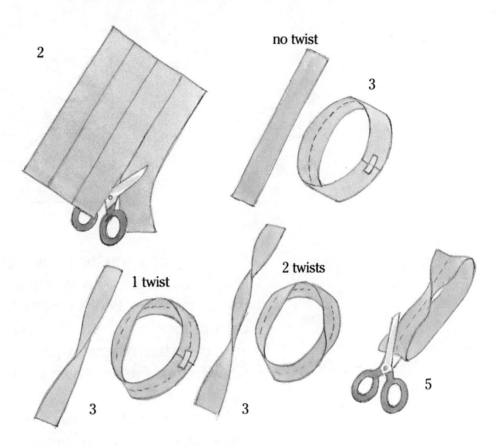

2 Cut the paper into strips along the lines.
3 Make the three different kinds of loops, as shown.
4 Tape the ends.
5 Cut the loops in half.

More twist fun: Make the same kinds of loops as above, but do not cut them in half. Cut one-third of the way in and keep on cutting.

JIGSAW PUZZLES   Make your own jigsaw puzzle. You'll need scissors, heavy paper, glue or paste, a pen, and a picture of something you like.

1 Spread a thin coat of glue on the heavy paper.

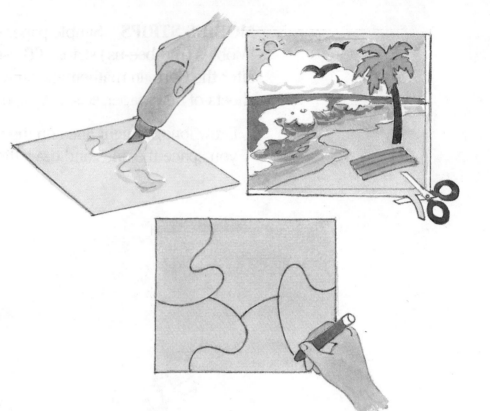

2 Put your picture on the gluey paper and press it smooth.

3 Dry the paper flat by covering it with newspaper or wax paper and laying books on top. Let the papers dry for one day or more.

4 Trim the edges of your paper.

5 Draw four or five lines over the back side of your paper.

6 Cut apart.

7 Try to put your puzzle back together.

8 Store the pieces of your puzzle in an envelope for safekeeping.

More to do: Trade puzzles with friends. Are some easier to put together than others? What makes a jigsaw puzzle hard to complete?

TIME NUMBERS   Numbers are very important for telling time. Do a time activity on page 111.

MONEY NUMBERS   You need to know about numbers to be able to use money smartly. Do a money activity on page 113.

NATURE SHAPES   There are many shapes in nature. Do the nature shape hunt on page 123.

COLORS AND SHAPES

Artists use colors, lines, and shapes to make art. Try these activities to make your own art.

POTATO STAMPER   Make a simple stamper. Potatoes are good to use for making your first stamps because they are easy to cut and will fit into your hand. You'll need a potato, a felt-tip pen, a flat dish with poster paint or a stamp pad, large sheets of paper, and a small knife.

1 Cut the potato in half.

2 With the felt-tip pen, draw a simple design on the potato.
3 With the tip of a small knife, cut on the lines you drew. Carefully cut the potato from around the outside part of the design. Your design will be higher than the part of the potato around the design.
4 Press the design onto the stamp pad or into the paint.
5 Press on paper.
6 Now you can see what one stamp design looks like. Use your stamper to make a bigger design.

COLORS AND SHAPES MOBILE   A mobile is a work of art made up of shapes that can move. Try making your own simple mobile. You'll need long plastic drinking straws, a large needle, thick thread, cardboard, paints, and crayons or markers.

1 Thread the needle and tie a knot in the end of the thread.

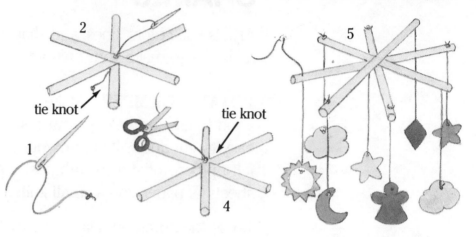

2 Poke the needle through the straws to attach them. Use three, four, or five straws.
3 Tie a knot in the thread near the straws.
4 Cut the thread, leaving enough for you to hang the mobile.
5 Add colored shapes, which you can cut from the cardboard and paint, to your mobile by attaching them to the straws with a needle and thread. Hang them at different lengths.
6 Your mobile may tell a story or be on a subject that interests you. See the illustration for ideas.
7 Have someone help you balance your mobile.

MAKING DOUGH SHAPES   You can mold and shape dough that you make yourself. You will need 1 cup cornstarch, 1 cup salt, 1$\frac{1}{2}$ cups flour, water, a mixing bowl, and a spoon.

1 Put the cup of cornstarch, cup of salt, and 1$\frac{1}{2}$ cups of flour in the bowl.
2 Stir.
3 Add $\frac{1}{2}$ cup of water and stir.
4 If the dough is still too stiff and dry, add one or two spoonfuls of water and mix with your hands.
5 You can make something with your dough after it is mixed, or you can save it for about two days. To save your dough, put it into a plastic bag. Close the bag and keep it in a refrigerator until you are ready to use it.

6 Make something with your dough. Here are some ideas. Roll pieces of the dough into little balls of different sizes. Put the balls together to make things. Rub a little water on the balls to help them stick.

OR

Start with one ball the size of a lemon, and pull and pinch the clay to make a shape—an animal or a building, for example.

OR

Roll the dough into a ball that fits into your hand. Press your thumbs into the middle of the ball. Press the hole bigger with one thumb while you turn the dough with the other hand. Keep doing this until the dough forms a pot or bowl shape.

WEAVING COLOR PATTERNS This exercise will teach you how to make patterns by weaving colors together. You'll need sheets of different-colored paper, scissors, ruler, clear tape, and a pencil.

1 Using the ruler, draw lines the length of the colored paper.
2 Space the lines the width of the ruler.

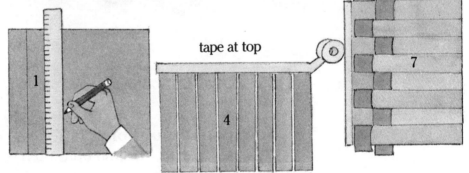

tape at top

make strips close together and even

3 Cut the paper on the lines to make strips.
4 Lay eight or more strips of the same color next to each other evenly.
5 Tape them together very close to the top.
6 Take eight strips of another color.
7 One at a time, weave the strips in and out, as the picture shows.

171

8 If the first weave started on top in the previous row, start it on the bottom in the next row.

9 After you have woven all the strips, cut the extra edges and tape them together.

10 Turn your finished weaving over to see how it looks without the tape showing.

More to do: Try weaving with more than eight strips. Try using more than two colors. Mix your strips to make different patterns. Try this with strips of fabric.

COLLAGES Collages are compositions made by pasting different items on a picture surface. Photos, drawings, fabric, string, and many other things all make up the composition. The many elements together show what the artist was thinking and feeling.

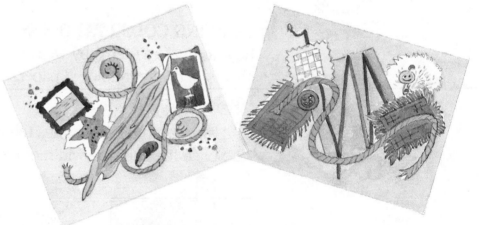

Make a collage to go with the activities on page 123.

A Rainbow of Colors You can mix your own colors. To learn how, try making your own painting. Start with only three colors. You'll need poster paint or tempera in red, blue, and yellow; paper cups; a paintbrush; paper; and a teaspoon.

1 Mix your three primary colors to form others. Follow this guide when you are ready to mix a color:

    red + blue = purple
    blue + yellow = green
    yellow + red = orange
    red + blue + yellow = brown

2 Put two teaspoons of each of the colors you need in a cup and stir.

3 After you have mixed the colors, you are ready to paint.

4 Paint a picture.

More to do: Use black and white paint to make a greater range of color.

red + white = pink
blue + black = dark blue

WORLD of THE ARTS

MUSIC

Music is the art of making sounds that are pleasing to the ear. Some sounds in nature, like birdcalls, are musical. You can make your own music.

MOVE TO THE MUSIC   Your body can tell the story of a song through movement. You will need records or tapes of different kinds of music—music that is fast; music that is slow; music with lots of instruments or voices; music with only one instrument or voice.

1 Listen to a variety of music. Find one song that you really like.

2 If you are listening to music without lyrics, make up a story to go with it.

3 Act out the story through dance while the music is playing.

MELODY GLASSES   Drinking glasses filled with different amounts of water can become a musical instrument. You will need eight same-size drinking glasses, water, and a spoon.

1 Number the glasses from one through eight.

2 Fill each glass with the amount of water shown in the picture.

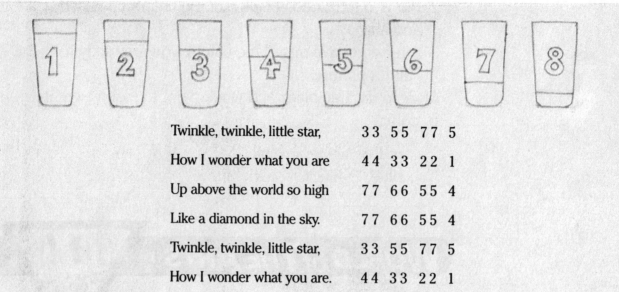

Twinkle, twinkle, little star,	33 55 77 5
How I wonder what you are	44 33 22 1
Up above the world so high	77 66 55 4
Like a diamond in the sky.	77 66 55 4
Twinkle, twinkle, little star,	33 55 77 5
How I wonder what you are.	44 33 22 1

3 Play "Twinkle, Twinkle, Little Star" on your melody glasses. The numbers above tell which glasses to tap. If a note doesn't sound just right, try adding or taking away a little water. Tap fast or slow in different places to follow the rhythm.

SINGING IN ROUNDS To sing in rounds, groups start singing a song at different times. You will need two groups of girls.

1 Practice singing the song "Make New Friends" until you know it well.

2 Now sing the song in parts. Group A sings the first line. When Group A begins the second line, Group B begins the

first line of the song. Group A finishes the second line and returns to the first line. The two groups will always be singing different parts of the song. You can stop at any time.

ACTION SONGS When you put motions, words, and music together, you have an action song. You will need someone to teach you an action song, or a tape or record of an action song. "The Brownie Smile Song" on page 14 has actions that go with the words. "Bingo" is an old folk song that also has rhythm actions to go with it.

1 Learn an action song and the motions. Here are the words to "Bingo."

> "Mary had a little dog and Bingo was his name.
> B-I-N-G-O, B-I-N-G-O, B-I-N-G-O (Sing each letter.)
> Bingo was his name."

2 The action in action songs takes the place of the word or is done with the word. Clap instead of saying the letters that spell "Bingo." Each time you sing the song, do one more clap and say one less letter, starting with "B."

3 Practice an action song with someone who knows the words and actions.

4 Perform your action song.

Bingo

Mar - y had a lit - tle dog and Bin - go was his name, Sir. B - I - N - G - O B - I - N - G - O B - I - N - G - O Bin - go was his name, Sir.

MUSIC FROM MANY CULTURES You can learn about another culture through its music. Read pages 90–93 in "My World." Learn two of the songs on pages 90–92.

EXERCISE TO MUSIC Music makes exercise fun. See page 55 in "Taking Care of Myself." Do the fitness wheel activity to music.

WORLD of THE ARTS

PUPPETS, DOLLS, AND PLAYS

Making puppets and dolls is an art. You can use them in plays or stories.

YARN DOLL These dolls are easy to make and you can add your own ideas. You'll need yarn or heavy thread, a small Ping-Pong ball or small round pebble, ribbons, cloth scraps, buttons, and other materials.

1 Cut yarn into strips the length of this page.
2 Make enough strips to fill your hand.

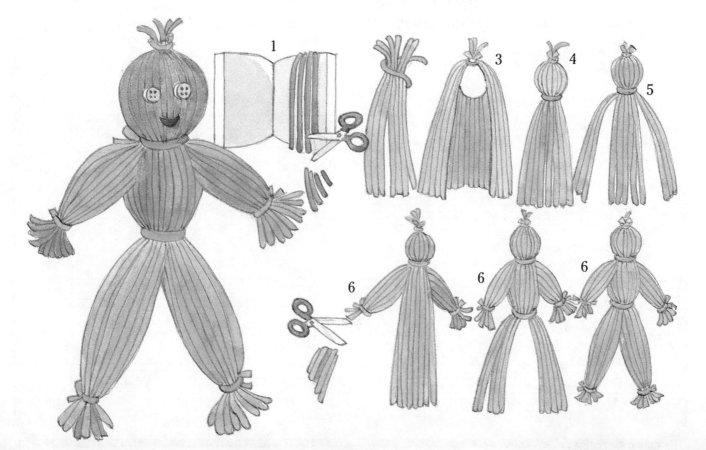

3 Tie all the strips together at the top.
4 Insert a Ping-Pong ball, wad of tissue, or pebble to give shape to the head.
5 Tie another string on the bottom of the ball, tissue, or pebble to make a neck.
6 Make arms and legs and a waist, as the drawing shows.
7 Use cloth and ribbons to dress the doll.

FINGER PUPPETS Turn the fingers of gloves into little puppets. Then put on a play. You'll need an old cloth or knitted glove, pieces of ribbon, string, thread, yarn, glue, strips of old material, markers, small buttons, beads, and tissue paper.

1 Make five grape-sized balls with the tissue paper, and stuff one into each finger of the glove.
2 Tie a piece of ribbon or yarn under the tissue ball.
3 Put a face on the finger tip with the markers, or sew or glue on buttons or beads.
4 Glue threads or yarn on the tip of the finger for hair.
5 Use yarn and scraps of cloth to dress your puppet.
6 Play with your finger puppets.

PAPER-BAG PUPPET Try making these easy puppets. You'll need small paper bags, pieces of paper, crayons, markers or paint, scissors, and glue.

1 Place the paper bag flat on a table with the bottom fold on top.
2 Draw and color designs on the bottom fold of the bag, which will be the head of your puppet. You can add eyes, ears, and hair.
3 Decorate the rest of the bag.

MARIONETTE There are string puppets as well as hand puppets. String puppets are called "marionettes." Try making this marionette. You'll need cardboard, string, beads or buttons, a stick or dowel, crayons or paints, paper, glue, a big needle, and heavy thread.

1 Cut the cardboard into an animal or human shape. Make a head, body, arms, and legs.

2 Color the pieces.

3 With the needle, poke four holes in the body for the arms and legs. Then poke a hole at the top of each arm and leg. Thread the needle and use it to tie together each leg and arm to the body.

4 Make a hole for the head at the top of the body.

5 Attach the head to the body by threading the hole. Tie a knot and cut the string.

6 Tie another string to the top of the head. To make your puppet move, raise and lower it by holding the string.

or

7 Tie a string to each arm and leg. Then tie these strings to two sticks tied in a cross.

8 Make your marionette walk and dance by moving the sticks.

A PUPPET STAGE   A stage will make a puppet show much more fun. You can make a stage for your puppets very easily.

For a curtain, you'll need one of the following: a sheet, a

towel, an old curtain, a tablecloth, or a piece of fabric. For a stage, you'll need a large cardboard box, a table on its side, a doorway, and two chairs. For ideas for a curtain and a stage, see the illustrations.

For scenery, you'll need cardboard, paper, paint, crayons, and markers.

1 Cut out shapes from the cardboard—trees and buildings, for example—and color them.
2 You can build simple buildings by cutting stiff paper into wide strips, taping them into circles, cutting a slit in the circles, and hooking them together.

SAFETY PLAY Put on a play or a puppet show about the safety do's and don'ts on pages 99–101.

WORLD of THE OUT-OF-DOORS

PLANTS AND ANIMALS

Plants and animals are the living things on this planet. There are many thousands of different kinds of plants and animals known to exist on earth. Try these activities to learn something about them.

SEED SPROUT Seeds are the beginnings of new plants. Water helps them grow. Watch how a seed sprouts. You'll need a clean glass jar with the label taken off, a paper towel, two or three seeds, and water.

1 Fold the paper towel in half. Roll the paper towel into a tube so you can insert it in the jar.
2 When you let go, the towel should press against the sides of the jar.
3 Add water to the jar so that it is as high as your thumbnail.
4 Poke seeds between the towel and jar, using a spoon or fork. Don't let the seeds fall into the water.
5 Check your seeds every day to watch them grow. Be sure there is always some water in the jar.

Something else to try: Do the same experiment with different seeds to see how they grow. Use corn, lima bean, green bean, squash, pumpkin, grapefruit, apple, or orange seeds.

SIMPLE PLANTS Mold is a very simple plant made up of many spores and is part of the fungus family. These spores are like very small seeds. They grow into mold and are in the air, soil, and dust.

Grow some mold. You'll need a small piece of bread, metal-foil wrap, a paper towel or napkin, and a magnifying glass (if you have one).

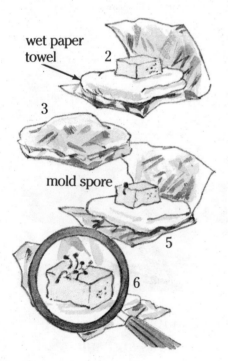

wet paper towel

mold spore

1 Get spores by waving bread in the air or sprinkling it with small amounts of dust.
2 Fold a piece of paper towel. Wet it with water.
3 Put bread on top of the paper towel. Wrap the towel and bread completely in the foil to keep it wet.
4 Place the wrapped bread in a dark spot.
5 Check the bread day by day to see what happens. Rewrap it after checking. (If you must wait a week before you can check the bread, sprinkle it with a few drops of water before wrapping.) Use a toothpick to move the bread. Wash your hands after looking at the mold.
6 Look at the colors and shapes of the growing molds. Most will be white and cottony, but there are many different types. As mold grows, it becomes powdery or has small dark dots

on it. These are new spores. A magnifying glass is very helpful for seeing the different shapes of mold.

Find out more about the helpful uses of mold, such as in the making of cheese or medicine. Learn why we wrap foods.

FOOD CHAIN   Plants make food for all living things and use the sun's energy to grow. When animals eat plants, they get energy. You get energy from eating food. Your food may be from plants or animals. A food chain shows how food energy is passed from one living thing to another. All food chains start with plant life.

To make a food chain, you'll need paper the size of this page cut in half the long way, crayons, pencils, tape, and pictures of plants and animals.

1 Pick a picture of a plant, or draw one. Tape it to a strip of paper.
2 With a piece of tape, loop the ends of the paper together. You now have the first link in your food chain.
3 Find or draw a picture of something that can eat your plant. Tape this to a new strip of paper. Loop the strip through the first link and tape the ends. Now your food chain has two links.
4 Find or draw a picture of something that can eat your second link, and make a third loop as in step three.
5 Keep going. Here are some food chain ideas for you to start with:

> corn—insect—small bird—fox.
> acorn—squirrel—hawk.
> flower—beetle—skunk—great horned owl.
> pond lily—water insect—frog—fish—other.
> grass—cow—you!

RABBIT WITHOUT A HOUSE   Many games children play are named after animals or are about the way animals live and act. Learn how to play the Brazilian game called Rabbit without a House. See page 89 for directions.

ADOPT A TREE   Do the adopt-a-tree activity on page 83 in the chapter "My World."

181

HABITAT HUNT   Every plant and animal has its own living place, called a "habitat." Do the habitat hunt on page 125.

WORLD of THE OUT-OF-DOORS

OUTDOOR FUN

Girl Scouts have fun doing things in and learning about the out-of-doors. These activities will help you learn and practice new skills and become an outdoor discoverer.

TOUCH, SMELL, LISTEN   You can learn about the outside world with all your senses. In this hunt, you will use more than your eyes to learn about the out-of-doors. You'll need your handbook and a pencil.

What to do: Find the things in the out-of-doors that match the descriptions on this list. Try to find more than one. Try to find things that are not on the list. After you find something, touch it and smell it to find out more about it.

TOUCH LIST	SMELL LIST	LISTEN LIST
1 something rough	1 something sweet-smelling	1 leaves rustling
2 something smooth	2 something sour-smelling	2 birds singing
3 something dull	3 something flowery	3 birds flying
4 something pointy	4 something minty	4 animals moving
5 something soft	5 something bad-smelling	5 water running
6 something hard	6 something pinelike	6 insects chirping
7 something bumpy	7 something lemony	7 wind moving things
8 something squishy	8 something fruity	
9 something crumbly		
10 something wet		

TRAIL SIGNS   Trail signs form shapes that show you which way to go and what to do on a trail. Learn how to make and use the trail signs that are on page 126 of the chapter "Things to Know."

ECOLOGY HUNT   "Ecology" (ee-kol-o-gee) is the study of living things—plants and animals—and their environment, their place on earth.

Try to find the things on the list below. You'll need your handbook and a pencil. You may or may not be able to find everything. When you find an item, check it on the list. This is a look-and-see hunt. Do your best not to disturb anything. Many plants are food or homes for other living creatures, so be careful as you explore.

1 worm	12 leaf with worm or insect holes
2 ant	13 pine needle
3 caterpillar	14 mushroom or fungus
4 snail	15 moss
5 butterfly or moth	16 flower
6 beetle	17 cactus
7 spider web	18 feather
8 squirrel	19 white grain of sand
9 animal footprint	20 smooth rock
10 seed	21 shiny, glassy rock
11 leaf with pointy edges	22 rock with many colors

More to try: Do this hunt at different times of the year. Make up your own list of things you found. Trade your list of things to hunt and find with friends.

RUBBINGS   A rubbing is one way to bring home something from the out-of-doors without disturbing nature. Check the following lists to see what are and are not good for rubbings:

GOOD	NOT GOOD
1 tree bark	1 living creatures
2 leaves	2 flowers
3 sand	3 very soft things
4 flat stones	
5 pine needles	
6 large rocks	

You'll need crayons and plain white paper.

1 Lay your paper against the thing from which you want a rubbing.

2 Gently rub a crayon back and forth until a pattern starts to show.
3 Do any of your rubbing patterns look alike? Try to collect many different patterns.
4 Show your rubbings to others. See if they can guess what your rubbings are.

KNOTS   Knots are very useful in the out-of-doors. Learn how to make the overhand and square knots. Read the directions on page 127 and make each knot.

OUTDOOR SNACKS   Make the fruit-and-nut mix or the walking salad snack to take on an outing. Follow the directions on page 129 to make them.

WORLD of THE OUT-OF-DOORS

OUTDOOR HAPPENINGS

It is fun to see how and why things happen outdoors. Try these activities to learn more about outdoor happenings like seed sprouts in the spring and morning dew.

SEED RACE   Seeds take different amounts of time to grow. Try this experiment to see which seed wins a sprout race. You'll need six kinds of seeds, one egg carton split in half, toothpicks, strips of paper, glue, potting soil, and water.

1 Take one, two, or three seeds from each of the packages. Be careful not to mix them together.
2 Write the name of each kind of seed on a strip of paper.
3 Glue the paper strips onto toothpicks. Be sure to keep each label next to its seeds.
4 Fill each section of the egg carton with about two tablespoons of potting soil.
5 Put one kind of seed in each section. You will have six sections, each with a different kind of seed.

6 Cover the seeds with more soil, and fill the section hole.

7 Stick your toothpick with the attached label in the soil.

8 Sprinkle with water.

9 Add a teaspoon of water every day.

10 Note which seeds show first. Watch them as they grow. You will see your seeds grow at different rates.

11 Try planting your sprouted seeds outside.

Find out more about growing things by reading books on gardening and by asking adults who have gardens about seeds.

FOSSIL PRINTS   Animals and plants that lived a very long time ago very often left prints in soft mud. After many years, these prints hardened into stone. Now, many years later, scientists are finding these prints. These prints and remains are called "fossils."

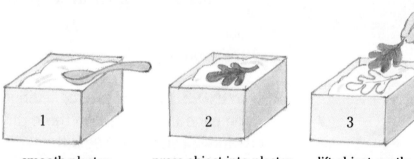

smooth plaster   press object into plaster   lift object gently

Try this experiment to see how prints made on soft, wet mud can harden. You'll need plaster of paris, a Styrofoam plate or the two-inch bottom of a paper milk container, and something to imprint (leaf, feather, piece of bark, etc.). You can even use your hand as a hand print.

1 Have someone help you mix the plaster and fill the container or plate. Be careful not to make the plaster too wet.

2 Lay the thing that you are going to imprint on the moist plaster.

3 Gently press on the whole piece and leave it for $1^1/_2$ minutes.

4 Lift it carefully and leave the plaster to dry.

5 If plaster sticks to the object, clean it.

6 Give your fossil to a friend or family member.

Find out about fossils and dinosaur tracks. Borrow books from your library on dinosaurs and other extinct creatures.

DEW MAKER   Water is in the air, but you can't see it. When the air cools, this water will sometimes settle on the ground. These drops of water are called "dew." You can make some of this water form by following the directions below. You'll need a clean, dry metal can without the label, ice cubes, and cold water.

1 Fill the can with ice cubes.

2 Add cold water.

3 Let the can sit for 30 minutes.

4 Check for dew on the outside of the can.

5 If it is very dry where you live, there may not be enough water in the air for the dew to form.

Something else to do: Notice what time of day you see dew on the ground.

WIND SPEED   Practice telling wind speed by using the chart on page 117. Go out on three different days and look for wind-speed clues. See if the wind changes from day to day.

WATCHING RAIN AND WHAT IT DOES   Do the rain-watching activity on page 118 of the chapter "Things to Know."

ROCKS   In the out-of-doors, you can find many kinds of rocks. One kind are formed by mud and sand and other things hardening. They are "sedimentary" (said-ah-men-ta-ree) rocks. Try this experiment to see how they form. You'll need pebbles, sand, pieces of rock, dirt, plaster of paris, water, and a paper cup.

1/2 cup

1

PLASTER of PARIS

1 tsp.

2

stir

3

peel away cup

5

1 Have someone help you mix the plaster in the paper cup. Make 1/2 cup.
2 Measure one teaspoon of pebbles, sand, dirt, and rock pieces.
3 Stir into the plaster.
4 Let the plaster mix dry.
5 Peel away the paper cup.
6 See if you can find a natural rock that looks like the one you made.

More to do: Start a rock collection.

INDEX